"Adolescence is a time of overdeveloped bodies and underdeveloped emotions." And would you believe there are people around who think it doesn't hurt?

Fred Hartley **knows** it hurts. He knows the pain is real. He knows the pressures and the choices you face every day are numerous and conflicting. He knows how overwhelmed you may feel, because he felt the same way himself, just a few years ago.

In this book, Fred shares with you his feelings about that time and his convictions about how you can make these years work for you—and feel good about yourself in the process.

BY FRED HARTLEY:

Update
Dare to Be Different
Growing Pains: First Aid for Teenagers

Growing Pains
First Aid for Teenagers

Fred Hartley

Illustrations by Gene Haulenbeek

Fleming H. Revell Company
Old Tappan, New Jersey

Library of Congress Cataloging in Publication Data
Hartley, Fred.
   Growing pains.
   1. Youth—Religious life. 2. Youth—Conduct of life. I. Haulenbeek, Gene. II. Title.
BV4531.2.H35   248.8'3   81-11952
ISBN 0-8007-5067-5   AACR2

WITH LOVE,
to mom and dad,
who patiently helped me through my growing pains

Contents

Introduction: Teenage Tears

Growing up means that you are supposed to act like an adult, even though sometimes you just feel like a big kid. Adolescence is a time of overdeveloped bodies and underdeveloped emotions. A life is never so exposed to pain and yet so unprepared to handle it as during the teenage years. I don't care if you're confronted with your newly divorced parents, breaking up with your boyfriend, or with the death of the family dog, growing up brings a bundle of pain.

Many people think teenagers don't hurt; others believe that if teens do hurt, they can handle it. We all know that our macho society demands we have the hide of a rhinoceros and the emotional stability of a steel girder. I've got news for you: Teenagers feel everything that a full-grown adult feels, but they are *not* equipped to handle it. Almost every day they are exposed to pains and pressures they have no idea how to respond to, and some kids are totally overwhelmed.

An adult body is said to have over 40 miles of nerves. For a teenager that often means 211,200 feet of frazzles.

Some kids live sheltered lives, while others grow up on battlefields. In either case, to make it through adolescence without getting hurt—and sometimes hurt seriously—is an impossibility. You show me someone who has never felt pain, and to borrow a phrase from Han Solo, I'll show you a "fuzzball."

Young Emotions

Adolescence is a time when we experiment and try new things, but moving into new areas of life usually causes pain and insecurity. The first day of high school usually brings a swarm of butterflies to teenage stomachs. Then there is the first day of football or cross-country practice, when many kids feel as though their lives are on the line. I always feared the first report card. The first night away from home at a summer camp or the first night alone in the hospital has turned many young men into mice, when they see their parents turn and walk out of the room. We often blame homesickness on the food or on the sleeping conditions, but there is obviously more to it than that.

When I went out for freshman football, I can remember thinking that I must have been the only nervous kid getting my helmet and pads. Even though I was one of the biggest kids on the team, on that first day, inside my belly, I felt small. Looking back, I can imagine what some of the smaller kids were saying to themselves as they looked at me: *Aw, man, what am I doing out here? Look at the size of him! I'll get killed or something!* When I was getting my gear, I thought I was the only fearful guy, when in fact the whole room was full of fear and apprehension.

Feelings of fear, inner pain, and even self-hatred and insecurity are not weird. They are normal. Every healthy teenager feels them. The important thing is that we accept them and learn to handle them, so that they do not mishandle us.

Common Pain

There are many sources of common pain; but regardless of the cause of our hurt, we are usually not prepared to handle it. The younger we are, the less prepared we find ourselves.

The first pain I felt after making it through the birth canal was when my dog died. My family always had dogs, but my favorite was Beaver, a purebred cocker spaniel. He was smart and responded quickly to my training. "Sit," "lie down," "fetch," and "heel" were all learned effortlessly. All I had to say was, "Ball," and he would find it anywhere in the house. Every afternoon at three o'clock, he'd sit on our front lawn, waiting for me to get off the bus. He was my friend.

One year, when we returned from a winter vacation, my father went to the kennel to pick up Beaver. When he drove down the driveway and got out of the car, he did not have a dog, just a burlap sack bulging with a shape like my dog's. All I could do was lock my teeth together, turn, and run. I ran until I could not run anymore; then I hit my fist into a tree and my foot into a rock. Despondently I flopped on the ground, lifted my head to the clouds high above the treetops, and cried to what was at that point a very unfair, unfeeling, impersonal Being, *"Why?"* All I knew was that Beaver was dead. I did not have any answers, and I hurt.

The next pain I can remember was when my grandfather died, when I was in high school. I was incapable of understanding my reaction. The phone rang as my mother and I were sitting in the kitchen. "Oh, no!" she cried in pain and disbelief. Many hard, silent tears followed. Finally, "Okay, mom, I have Fred. We'll be right down." My mother put the receiver down and held her sobbing face in disbelief. It was not necessary for her to tell me, because the dagger of my grandfather's death had gone through her heart into mine. It felt a lot like the pain from Beaver's death, except now it was something bigger, more mysterious, because this time it involved a human life.

Faltering insecurities overwhelmed me as we drove the hour-long trip to my grandmother's house: *What do I say? I am not sure what I feel or that what I feel is right. Why was I able to cry more easily when Beaver died? That's stupid, don't even think that!* My mind raced on. My grandfather was a fishing buddy and a baseball buddy. He was a large authority figure for me, but he was also a friend. All the time we had spent together had caused us to stick, the way glue fastens paper together. The problem was, he was torn away from me, and my heart felt shredded; my brain was scarred with question marks, and again I did not have any answers.

Death is a common occurrence that causes deep pain to anyone who experiences it, but to a teenager who is innocent and unprepared, it can be overpowering.

Our society does not teach us how to handle death—or any pain, for that matter. In fact from our earliest years we are taught "Men do not cry, only babies cry." Parents mock tears with the harmful words, "Cry baby." They say, "Men don't cry!" (I always wondered what was wrong with Jesus, He cried.) The brilliant German pastor and theologian Helmut Thielicke, when asked about the supreme failure of our culture, replied, "They have an inadequate view of suffering."

This inadequate view of suffering and pain is seen in the song "Walking on Thin Ice," which Yoko Ono recorded with her husband the night he was fatally shot:

> I may cry some day
> But the tears will dry which ever way
> And when our hearts return to ashes
> It'll be just a story.

There must be more to tears than that!

If only a small percentage of the 25 million teenagers hurt, that would be one thing. However that is not the case. Adolescence is full of agonies; the only reason they are not more obvious is that teenagers have been taught that emotions such as sorrow, grief, anger, frustration, and depression are wrong. Pathetically many parents are not helping their young people deal with these feelings, and the results are devastating. When crying and confusion are belittled, it does not take kids long to bury such experiences and attempt to forget about them. Rejection and denial only cause worse problems. Millions of kids will be alone in bed this year and whisper to the darkness, "What's wrong with me? I hurt!"

Hard-Core Pain

We have all felt common pain. Common pain stings for a while, but then it goes away; we forget about it, and basically we go on unchanged.

Hard-core pain is different. It is much worse. Hard-core pain comes like a thief and reaches deep within our guts and yanks out something precious that we wanted more than anything on earth. It is the pain that makes us hate, driving young lives to drugs, sex, and booze. It has taken more lives than car accidents and world wars. It is not quite as common as *common pain,* but it occurs more frequently than most people realize. And its favorite targets are teenagers.

If you have ever felt hard-core pain, you will never again be the same. Some feel it when they are raped. Others feel it when a father or mother dies. Others feel it when their parents go through a divorce. Hard-core pain can be caused by hundreds of things, but it always involves something we love.

Dawn's life is a vivid example of the effects of hard-core pain. Childhood tragedy has mutilated her emotions. She is an alcoholic. She has lived a free and reckless life for the past several years, living with a big-time junkie, where she had as much cocaine as she wanted—about $300 worth a day. She has been raped by a motorcycle gang and abused by countless others. Both her arms show scars on top of scars, reminding her of times when she attempted suicide. The sex, the drugs, the booze, and the razor blade scars are all just on the surface. Underneath is hard-core pain.

The pain came to Dawn at an age when she was not prepared to handle it. Her parents were divorced before her fourth birthday, and she did not see her father again until she was much older, and then she saw him only briefly. Her mother was stunned by the divorce, and she turned to the bottle. When her mother gained a reputation as an alcoholic, schoolmates teased Dawn by calling her mother, the Tramp. She did not want to believe it, but Dawn knew much of it was true. Dawn can still remember having a chair broken over her head and then being carted from foster home to foster home. She was kicked around like a soccer ball and had the scars to prove it. She needed relief and looked to booze and drugs. She needed affection and looked to guys who wanted sex. Even though those things made her feel cheap and polluted, what difference did it make anyway? After all, she had always been treated like a piece of trash. What difference did it make to her to put a blade to her wrist? No one cared. No one else has ever cried over her. She felt about as valuable as a cigarette butt, and the only thing worth doing to a cigarette butt is putting it out.

There was nothing she wanted more than the love she never got from her parents, yet she was filled with bitterness and resentment toward them. She was well aware of the self-destructive effect drugs and alcohol were having on her, and yet no one had ever taught her that she was worth saving. And then God. . . . It was pretty hard for her to trust Someone who was supposed to be all-powerful and all-loving, when He had done such a lousy job with her life so far. If what had happened in her life was an example of God's love and control, forget it!

I love Dawn as if she were my own daughter. And I care about the thousands of others just like her, throughout the country, who have been treated like trash and who have suffered from hard-core pain.

Your life might be very different from Dawn's. But you probably stand in part of her shadow. The source of pain might be entirely different, and the intensity might be less, but pain is pain! What would be like gasoline in the eyes to one might be like water off a duck's back to another. In the same way, what means nothing to someone else might cause your whole world to crumble. Hard-core pain is identified, not by the size of the cause, but by the effect. Regardless of the cause, when it is felt, pain is pain. Teenage tears are usually unnoticed, except when they are rolling down your own cheeks. Because no understanding or compassion is shown at these insecure moments, you can become fully convinced that you are either weird or worthless.

A man who has gone down in history as the wisest man who ever lived, Solomon, cared a lot about teenagers. Much of the insight he gives is specifically directed toward young people. Approximately three thousand years ago he wrote:

> Young people, enjoy your youth.
> Be happy while you are still young. . . .

> Don't let anything worry you
> or cause you pain.
> You aren't going to be young
> very long.
>
> Ecclesiastes 11:9, 10 TEV

In the pages to follow we will look at many of the things that have caused you pain. I hope it will be like looking into a mirror. This book is designed to help you through the minefield of teenage life so that you can avoid many of the casualties others have faced and keep your life from ending up in the junkyard.

A Final Question

Before we leave this chapter: Do you have the guts to admit you cry? Or if you do not cry, will you at least admit that at times you feel like it? Can you admit that there are things that hurt you? things that make you scared and insecure? things that you lie awake at night, thinking about, worrying about, stewing over? If you live with only one of your parents, have broken up with a boyfriend, or have been cut from the basketball team, you probably know what I am talking about.

Be honest. Let those feelings you have been hiding in the closet come out for a while. No one is going to tell you you are weird or call you a cry baby. Teenage tears are okay. After all, Jesus said, "Blessed are those who weep, for they shall be comforted" (*see* Matthew 5:4).

I am well aware that hurts and pains and problems are all things that make us feel weak, and they are awkward to talk about. In fact they are easy to run from and deny altogether; if that is where you are at, you might as well close the book or prove how strong you are by tearing it in half. On the other hand, if honesty does not frighten you and if you are aware of some hurts in your own life that you have not been able to figure out, keep reading.

1. What was the first major pain you can remember?
2. Do you know anyone like Dawn? What words can you use to describe his or her life? In what ways have you felt like her?
3. When you get hurt, how do you respond? (a) talk about it; (b) withdraw, feel sorry for myself; (c) get stoned; (d) _____.

1. Have you ever lost a dog or family member? How did it make you feel at first?
2. Make a list of some pains, frustrations, and conflicts that teenagers face.
3. Tell the group about the last time you cried (if you have the guts).
4. Why don't we like to admit that we have weaknesses?

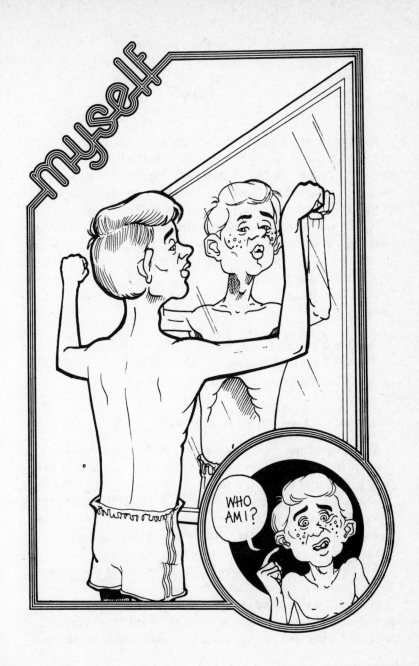

1 "Toads"

Have you ever felt like a toad? Have your friends ever seemed to avoid you as if they were afraid that they might break out in warts if they got too close? Have you felt like a failure at the things you have tried and concluded that you are a worthless creature? Then join 25 million other insecure teenagers, who feel the same way.

We all need to feel good about ourselves; we need to be worth something to someone; we need a sense of self-respect and human dignity. We all want to be important, but the problem is, we usually look to the wrong places.

Let's look at the three most common areas where people find self-respect:

1. What I look like (my face)
2. What I do (my name)
3. What others say about me (my fame)

I Am What I Look Like (My Face)

As young people, we grow to love or hate our bodies very quickly. But no matter who you are, it is very easy to find some flaw. Either your breasts are too small or your thighs are too fat. Your hair looks like a Brillo pad or your skin looks like the bark on a tree. Freckles, zits, moles, scars, and facial hair all work against teenagers. Guys often suffer from being too short and girls from being too tall.

What about you? Is there anything that you would change about your appearance if you were able?

I knew a girl who hated the kinky curls in her hair. During junior high she made herself look ugly just because she hated her hair so much and concluded that she was a lost cause. When the Afro permanents came in style, she was exhilarated; what God gave her originally was now what people were paying money for.

A friend of mine was always shorter than the rest of us. His father was five foot two inches and his mother, four foot ten inches. In high school his height kept him from most athletics, and he deeply resented the fact that his family was so short. When platform shoes came in, he was the first one out to buy them, but then when they went out of style, he could never kick the habit. To this day he still wears four-inch platform shoes.

Television, glamour magazines, and movies all portray the image that only blond beauties have fun. Unless you have a cover-girl smile or a muscular body, you are a nobody. The ironic thing is that even the "beautiful people" hate certain things about themselves. Just listen to what *Seventeen* magazine (August 1980, p. 336) said these famous females think about themselves:

- Suzanne Somers thinks her legs are too thin.
- Linda Ronstadt says she looks awful in photographs.
- Lauren Hutton, the Revlon model, thinks her nose is crooked and her face is asymmetrical.
- Kristy McNichol hates her nose.
- Linda Gray, who plays Sue Ellen Ewing on the TV show "Dallas," recalls being teased for her "bug eyes" as a teenager.
- Jayne Kennedy, former beauty queen and CBS sportscaster, spent years regretting how tall she is.
- Valerie Bertinelli, famous TV star, hates her thighs.

Yes, even the beautiful people hate certain things about themselves. The interesting thing about those listed here is that many of them—if not all—began to resent those parts of their bodies during their teenage years.

In some ways the beautiful people have it worse than the rest of us: Frequently they have built careers on physical beauty. Their identities are wrapped up in being "pretty faces." What happens when they get old and wrinkled or if they suffer accidents in which they are scarred? Their personal worth is gone, and their sense of dignity has been destroyed. If even the beautiful people see flaws in their physical beauty, we might conclude that there is no hope for us.

There are certain things you can do to help your physical appearance. For $2,000 you can get a nose job; for $1,500 you can have the bags under your eyes removed; for $750 you can pin your ears back, if they stick out too far; if you want your fat neck trimmed down, it will cost you $2,750; for $750 you can get any wrinkles out of your forehead; and for a meager $500 they can change the shape of your mouth.

It does not cost anything to go on a diet so you do not feel like a fat pig, and if you avoid chocolate and peanut butter, it will certainly help your acne condition. But apart from plastic surgery and platform shoes, there is nothing you can do about certain things.

Fortunately, physical appearance was never intended to give us our sense of self-worth. Even those who do love themselves because of their physical beauty will always suffer from insecurity because their self-respect is based on something that can be taken away from them.

Let's keep looking.

I Am What I Do (My Name)

The second most popular place to look for self-worth is in natural ability. If I am superior in a skill, whether it be shooting baskets, playing the drums, or taking exams, then I have a tendency to see myself as a superior person. If, however, I am one of those less fortunate (and typical) teenagers who is just an ordinary athlete or just an ordinary musician or just an ordinary student, then I will often regard myself as a nobody.

Athletics.   In some schools, if you do not have a varsity letter, you do not have anything. That is the way it was for Bob. More than anything in the world, he wanted to play baseball. His father taught him many of the skills as a young boy, and he caught on quickly. He could play any position, and he played them all well. He pitched his Little League team on to the championships and had one of the highest batting averages in the state. His coach had sent several boys to the minor leagues, but he had never seen anyone play baseball like Bob.

Bob was in a near-fatal accident at the beginning of the summer. What bothered him, as much as almost losing his life, was missing a summer of baseball. A year later he got involved in a city-league team and amazed all the other players and coaches with his natural ability. One night he hopped on his girl friend's bike and headed down the road to get some pop. Two cars were drag racing. One swerved six feet off the road, hit Bob's bike, and sent him flying over the windshield like a wounded bird. He lay unconscious until the police and ambulance came to his rescue.

Incoherent, Bob was taken to the hospital, where, two days later, they would remove his left leg, above the knee. When they cut off his leg, they cut off his potential baseball career; they cut off the one thing he did better than anything else. He had a name as a great baseball player. Now that name would only be memories—and small ones, compared to what might have been.

There are kids everywhere who have lost all respect for themselves because they had their athletic careers taken from them. For every person like Bob there are dozens who never had any self-respect because they did not make the team or because they spent all their time playing "left out." Athletics is an important area of teenage life. It is almost a requirement: If you cannot play sports, you just are not normal; there is something missing; you are not a complete person.

Intelligence.   In other schools, athletics are not as important as academics. We could call this the Almighty A. Competition for grades has created all kinds of psychological strain on young people who become fully convinced that they are not worth a Bic pen because, regardless of effort, they are B-minus students.

The college I attended, Wheaton College, was highly competitive. There was a great deal of emphasis put on academic excellence—in fact, so much so that to get a C on a paper or exam was like committing the unpardonable sin. Sophomore year I was taking a New Testament course from a professor everyone feared; he was known for exacting exams. So to prepare myself, I studied harder than I had ever studied for a single examination. For weeks I let my other subjects slip in order to concentrate on this test. The day of reckoning came. I walked in, sat down, prayed, and took the test. Four hours later I got up, found my girl friend, and took her out for a victory dinner, because I knew that I had "killed it." All my studying had paid off.

Two days later as we filed into class the corrected papers were on the professor's desk. Being precise, before he handed them back, on the blackboard he put a graph of all the different grades, with a breakdown of two 90s, nine 80s, twenty-five 70s, five 60s, and one 50. I was surprised that there were only two grades in the 90s, but I was confident that I had one of them. After all, I had studied more than anyone else, and my major was Bible. In almost cultic pageantry, he walked up and down the rows, silently handing out the papers. Expressionlessly he would place the papers facedown on the various desks, and as the students got them they would very slowly lift up the corner of the paper to see the grade and place it back down. Not me. When I got my paper, I flipped it over; in a sense I probably wanted everyone to see what I got. I could not believe it. I had to check my name to make sure that it was mine, and even then I was convinced that there must have been more than one Fred Hartley in the class. (You think I got the 50, but you are wrong.) I got a 60. I was crushed. I think I crawled out of the room. When I brought it to my girl friend, she did not know whether to laugh or cry. I could not do either. All emotion was gone. It took me three weeks to get back to normal, because I was convinced that I was *not* normal.

If you attend a school where there is fierce competition for grades, then perhaps you have felt worthless because your brain is not as big as someone else's. Well, I have good news for you: You were never intended to grade your personal worth on the basis of what your report card says, because a human being is more than a brain on top of a body.

There are countless other ways we judge ourselves according to our abilities: how well we make friends, whether or not we are able to make them laugh, or how quickly we learn to play a musical instrument. In some schools immorality is a status symbol. The amount of grass smoked, beer drunk or girls played with determines how much we are worth. Other areas place the premium on the ability to make money, regardless of whether it is made selling dope or stealing cars. Whatever ability is elevated, how we perform is frequently what we use to decide whether or not we are normal. However even our abilities are not worth building our self-esteem around. If I love myself just because of what I do, what happens when I cannot do it anymore? We still have not found a basis for our self-respect.

I Am What Others Say About Me (My Fame)

If you are anything like most members of the do-your-own-thing generation, you probably deny being affected by what others think about you. But whether or not we admit it, a major criterion for what we think of ourselves is what our friends think about us. Rejection and bitter criticism from friends have caused more pain to teenagers than arthritis has to the elderly.

John Lennon, the power droid of the most influential musical force of the sixties, the Beatles, was looked upon as a top guru of the do-your-own-thing philosophy. He was unquestionably a pacesetter, not only in music, but also in the religious thought of our generation. He was the prophet who certainly would not have been influenced by peer pressure, so we thought.

However, after five years of silence, during which he lived in his elegant seventh-floor Dakota apartment in New York with his wife, Yoko Ono, he cut an album entitled *Double Fantasy.* Just prior to its release he made a statement, only months before his untimely assassination, explaining his silence:

> I realized that I wasn't making records for me anymore, but because people and record companies expected me to. . . . Still it was hard for me to admit that I was allowing some illusion to control me. After all, wasn't I the great pop seer? Was I not the great John Lennon who could see through all the world's hypocrisy? The truth was I couldn't see through my own. It's easy to see thy neighbors and say, "You and your phoniness." The trick is to see your own.

The great John Lennon influenced and controlled by what others thought of him. *Yes,* even John Lennon.

John Lennon, although manipulated by public opinion, was not really being hurt or abused by it the way Eric was. Eric is a friend of mine who is also a guitar player and songwriter. But unlike John Lennon, Eric is a no-name.

Eric has played his heart out for four years of high school and for about six years before that. He is not a bad musician, but like most, he is nothing exceptional. I talked with Eric after he had tried, for the third straight year, to win the state competition and had failed. In years past he had consoled himself that there was always another year, but now he was a senior. He was at the end of the road, and he had come through empty. Thousands of hours of practice got him nowhere. He lay awake at night, thinking about finally being somebody.

Eric turned to look at me and said sadly, "See, I'm a nobody. Year after year I go there, thinking I'm *somebody,* and then I come back a *nobody.* This year I just hated going as the representative for our school, because I came back a failure. I never even made the school newspaper."

Eric was so convinced he was a worthless toad that I interrupted, "Who says you're a nobody?"

"Everybody! Everybody knows I'm worthless." Well, it was a sealed case for Eric. He was thoroughly convinced that his worthlessness was public knowledge, and that fact of being worthless in the eyes of others caused Eric great pain.

Eric had the problem many of us have: He compared himself to perfection, because he so wanted to be recognized by his friends. He wanted to be *the best.* He wanted a famous name for himself. Then having made such a perfect standard, he was unable to measure up. He made the ultimate seem like the norm, so when he failed to be the best, in his eyes he failed to be normal.

Perhaps one of the worst things for Eric was not being mocked and teased, because he really was not; the problem was that he just was not noticed. George Bernard Shaw perceptively said:

> The worst sin toward our fellow creatures is not to hate them, but to be indifferent to them: that's the essence of inhumanity.

Constantly thinking about what others think of us creates peer pressure, and that pressure is pain. It hurts to be skinny for weight lifting or fat in the showers. It hurts to be stupid when the papers are graded in class or brilliant when everyone else is jealous that you were on the honor roll.

Unfortunately, most of us accept what others say about us as the truth. If they say we are fat, then we are fat. If they say we are stupid, then we are stupid. If they say we are ugly, then we might as well throw in the mop. Even though it might contradict everything we have ever thought, what others say about us should not determine how we feel about ourselves. If we do base our self-respect on what others say about us, we will always suffer from insecurity, because no matter who we are, we will always have a critic.

Insecurity

Webster defines *insecurity* this way, "The state of being insecure; not safe from danger; feeling more anxiety than seems warranted; not firm or dependable; unreliable." We could define it more simply this way: "Building our lives around anything that can be taken away from us," as Bill Gothard has stated.

Insecurity always hurts. The trouble is, most of us do not know anything different from building our lives around temporal relationships. After all, we live in a temporal world with worn-out philosophies like "You only go around once in life, so grab for all the gusto you can get." We quickly learn that friends fail us, and our fame often becomes shame.

Do you ever feel like the little metal ball inside a pinball machine? When people come up and put a quarter in the machine, you bounce around from place to place, making bells go off and lights come on. You are on display, and the louder they cheer, and the harder they hit the machine, the faster you move. But when they are through with you or when their money runs out, there you are, back where you started—lying silent at the bottom of the machine, waiting in line while others take their turn.

For some of us that is all we have ever known. We have been bounced and kicked around like pinballs.

Mama Cass: A Case of Insecurity

In the late sixties the Mamas and the Papas were regarded as the single most successful music group of their time, with hits such as "Monday, Monday" and "California Dreamer." They zipped around the country in Lear Jets, spent money almost as fast as they made it, often traveling with fifteen or more friends, staying in the best hotels. They recklessly bought cars and houses. The members included Denny Doherty, John and Michelle Phillips, and of course the most noticeable, the fat mama, Cass Elliott.

Cass loved the luxury. After all, she could recall ten specific times when her father went bankrupt during her childhood, when she still went by her real name, Naomi Cohen.

While still in high school she got a part as a singer in a summer play. That gave her the recognition she had hungered for and launched her into the world of vocal fame as the flamboyant fat girl. She spent time singing in New York City, at nineteen, and then connected with the famous quartet.

The Mamas and the Papas appeared on the covers of many magazines and drew big crowds everywhere they went. Cass made friends with bellboys, waitresses in diners, and with stagehands. Her favorites, though, were the fat people. She had a soft place in her heart for the obese, and they flocked to her concerts like kids to candy. They loved her because she was fat, too, yet she was somebody.

Tragically Cass's career went way up and way down. She had her moments of stardom, but then there were those moments of tremendous humiliation. After she left the quartet, she tried to solo in Vegas, and she was forced to crash-land. It was such a bomb that *Newsweek* reported she blamed it on astrology: "I have been trying to struggle up when my planets have been pulling me down." Ironically, while at Caesar's Palace, in Las Vegas, she sang:

On your knees but unconquered, taxed beyond your strength,
Now you know the Prince of Darkness, will go to any length,
To keep you from flying, Flying too high.

At one point, according to *Esquire* magazine, she was the featured centerfold for the rock magazine *Cheetah.* She appeared naked, lying in a field of daisies, with various tattoos on her pink body. She almost looked like a huge, happy pig after a big meal.

There were certainly ugly moments for Mama Cass, which made her career a mixture of the glorious and the pathetic. Nothing so effectively illustrates this as the way things ended.

She was in London, staying in a luxurious city apartment, on Monday night, July 29, 1974. She lay in bed, watching TV and enjoying her most passionate pastime: eating. She had a ham sandwich and who knows what else. That next day the world read headlines: "Mama Cass Dead at 33." The report from her physician, which has since been brought into question, read, "probably choked to death on a ham sandwich," but it did not rule out the possibility of a heart attack.

In a sense the coroner's report did not much matter. All the public would remember was the fat mama reaching for just one more ham sandwich. Naomi Cohen, who had known so many humiliating moments, from childhood to stardom, was taken through a faltering fatality. All the fat-girl jokes she told seemed so grossly inappropriate. Such a life and death speak to us about the pathetic and mortal moments of life.

I have thought about all the obese who saw in Cass the hope that they, too, were worth something more than just another ham sandwich. All their dreams were popped like a hot-air balloon the morning of July 30, when they woke to the news that she was dead.

Regardless of whether we look to a famous individual to find our self-worth or just to a personal friend, we will usually be unfulfilled. If our personal worth depends on another person, then we are not worth much. Friendships based on such a need are highly fragile and will usually become highly painful.

2 "I'm Somebody"

God does not want us to feel like toads. If He did, He would have made us toads. He made us people, the highest form of His creation, and He wants us to feel important—every single one of us.

The reason we often feel unimportant and insecure is because we measure ourselves by the wrong yardsticks: physical beauty, natural talent, and public opinion. Those rulers swat our hind sides all the way through high school. Wouldn't it be great to crack all those yardsticks and be free from their severe discipline? That is what we are doing. We are destroying those false measuring sticks that make us feel small and inadequate. Under a new standard, we might even learn to love ourselves.

Did you realize that people who genuinely love themselves are not conceited? People who genuinely love themselves are Christians.

I'm Somebody 'Cause God Made Me

A few weeks ago I went up to Children's Variety Hospital, in Miami. As I walked to the front door, out was being wheeled a six-year-old girl who had no legs. I squeezed into the elevator, and next to me was a chrome cage; lying in the middle of that cage was an infant with numerous hoses draped from his face. As I pressed the button to take me to the sixth floor, I felt very uncomfortable. As I got off the elevator, I stepped aside for another young girl, struggling to walk with a cumbersome metal leg brace. I looked in the first room to see a mongoloid child. The next room held a newborn with open wounds on his oversized head. I felt uneasy, uncomfortable, and insecure. *How are these kids going to feel about themselves?* I thought. *What would it feel like to be one of them?* I watched a nurse change a severely burned seven-year-old who was thrashing about, and I again questioned, *How can they continue to live, when they look so deformed and ugly?* In my head I desperately tried to affirm that they, too, were created in the image of God and had immortal souls with eternal worth, but the environment stripped me of my theological education. It was like getting slapped in the face with a manta ray. I was stunned, and I stared, speechless. A nurse asked if she could help me, and I could not respond. As I walked past the nurse's station, I looked in at a poster that sent a ray of sunlight into my dark mind. On it was a saying I will never forget: I'M SOMEBODY 'CAUSE GOD DON'T MAKE NO JUNK. Immediately those eight words triggered within me a desire to communicate that message to hurting teenagers everywhere.

You might have been treated like a useless hunk of trash for your whole life, but I've got news for you: *You're somebody 'cause God don't make no junk!* It does not matter how much pain you have felt, you are not a piece of trash. You might hate your acne condition or your fat legs. You may have been cut from the varsity team or even flunked out of school. Your so-called friends might treat you like a toad, and your own parents might have taught you that you were less valuable than the evening newspaper, but I have news for you, "You're somebody 'cause God don't make no junk!"

I'm Somebody 'Cause Jesus Died for Me

Jim was a young man who always looked down on himself because he constantly compared himself to others. He never had a close friend outside his family, and even his parents never showed him much attention. To them he was just another mouth to feed. As a teenager he felt rejected and very insecure. He was not a bad student, but then he was nothing exceptional. He was not bad looking, but you could never convince him of that.

Sophomore year he moved into a new neighborhood, and the family next door gave him a lot of attention. There was a guy about his age in the family, who invited him to several activities. Jim's neighbor gave him a Bible to read and told him about God. At first Jim resisted the friendship, because he kept waiting for things to go wrong, the way all his other friendships had. But when nothing went wrong, he listened carefully. In reading the Bible, the parts that he reread the most told him about God's love. Jim felt comfortable enough to start telling his friend about his inner feelings of weakness and worthlessness. He had been so unloved and so unaccepted that he found it difficult to believe he was actually loved and accepted by God.

One night I went to Jim's house, and we looked through the Bible, reviewing verses about God's love. "All I believe is that a superhuman Being is out there somewhere. It is really hard for me to handle the idea that God wants to express personal love to me. Nobody has ever wanted to do that."

Why would he reject a personal, loving God? I asked myself. Then an idea popped into my head. "Jim, if you had the power, what would you change about yourself?" At first the question caught him off guard, so I gave him a few examples. "Well, you know, is there anything about yourself that you wished was different—like something about your physical features or any of your abilities?"

He gave me a half smile and admitted, "Yeah, I guess everyone has something. I have always hated not being able to make friends. It has always made me feel like a jerk. I am very self-critical. When I am at school or at my job, I get these weird thoughts that people hate me, even when they probably don't. If someone looks at me a little strangely, I think about it for days. I hate that about myself. I just wish I could be normal and make friends, like everybody else." When he paused, I told him I understood how he felt. Then he continued, "I just wish someone would accept me. I wish someone would love me for who I am. I hate trying to measure up."

As Jim talked it sounded as though he was describing Jesus, without using His name. "You know, there is One Person who knows everything about you, and yet He loves you anyway. He accepts you just the way you are, and He wants to be your Friend."

That evening we read a number of verses from the Bible. The final verse was this, "In this act we see what real love is: it is not our love for God, but his love for us when he sent his Son to satisfy God's anger against our sins (1 John 4:10 TLB).

That night as I left I did not know what was happening in Jim's head or in his heart. All I could do was pray. I knew it was hard for him to accept a loving God when he did not love himself. The next day he was sitting in a classroom all by himself. The same thoughts of self-criticism overcame him. *See, you idiot. Here you are all alone again. You don't have a friend in the world. No one has ever loved you, and they probably never will.*

"Stop it!" he cried, interrupting those worn-out thoughts. He pulled a little booklet from the back pocket of his jeans and reread some Bible verses that talked about God's love for him.

"Jesus, I want You," he said, putting his head down on the desk. "I want You to come into my life. I am sick of wandering through life like a stray dog. I believe that You died on the cross for my sins, to show me how much You love me, and that You rose from the dead and are alive right now! Please come into my life and be my Friend. I will do whatever You want me to, because if You made me and know everything about me, then You certainly know what is best for me. Thank You for showing me how much You love me."

He lifted his head from the desk, and suddenly he was not alone anymore. Neither was he unloved and unaccepted. He told me that he had never in his entire life felt such genuine joy. He literally ran from the classroom and went to find his neighbor-friend to tell what had happened. Jim knew that he was loved because of the Man who died on the Tree for him.

If you have never been touched by Jesus' love, He wants you to know that He loves you so much that He died for you. Perhaps no one has ever put his arms around you and told you that you are normal, but Jesus will if you will let Him. If you will open your heart, Jesus promises that He will come in and live with you (Revelation 3:20). He will show you that you are somebody.

I'm Somebody 'Cause He's Making Me Somebody

When Jesus first introduces Himself to us, inviting us to become part of His family, He says, "Come as you are." He does not require us to take a shower, to comb our hair (or get it cut), to change our clothes, or even change our language. He simply says, "Come." After we come, Jesus still respects our individuality. He made us unique, and He intends to keep us that way, but He does bring changes. If you expect to follow Jesus and remain the same, then you must be confused. Either you are not really following Jesus or you are a miserable individual, because Jesus is a Change Agent who guarantees to renovate our lives from the tip of our tongues to the bottom of our hearts. If we bear the name *Christian,* Jesus' name is at stake, and you can be confident that He is going to make us feel worthwhile and respectable.

As a teenager, sports were my life. In the fall I played football, in the winter I ran track, and in the spring I played baseball. My senior year I had aggressively prepared myself for football. Weighing 200 pounds, I was on the starting team of both the offensive and defensive squads—playing tight end and defensive end. One day I had made several good tackles on defense and caught several passes on offense. Near the end of the game, the other team had the ball on our five-yard line; five yards and they would win the game. The ball was snapped, pitched back to their fullback, who turned to run around my end. I was the only one there to stop the play. I lowered my head as I ran straight toward the ball carrier, and he lowered his as he ran toward me; we were like two locomotives on the same track! *Schmack!* I staggered off the field, dazed. A little smelling salts and I was fine—for almost five minutes.

We won the game, but physically I felt horrible. As time went on I felt worse and worse, until they put me in the hospital with what the doctors diagnosed as a minor concussion.

Hours turned into days, and my condition worsened. When my parents asked, "He's going to live through it, isn't he?" the neurologists were not able to say. Brain scans, spinal taps, and angiograms all revealed damage, but the full extent would only be revealed by whether or not I lived.

Thousands of sincere Christians, from my own church and in many other churches, prayed for me. The youth group I was a part of called a special prayer meeting for me. One night as I lay on the hospital mattress, screaming from pain, with tears flowing from my face and sweat from my body, nurses struggled to relieve me. My parents were asked to leave. I had hardly slept during the eight days I had been in the hospital, and I had only eaten a little pound cake. I was wasted. Before this I had tried to bargain with God, "You get me out of here, and I will give up drinking and dancing. I'll never curse again." But God was not interested in my bargains. He wanted my life.

My pulse dropped to twenty-six beats a minute. I felt my life teetering on the edge of eternity. I saw life, but I also saw death, and I knew that I could slip either way. I quit struggling. I quit bargaining. My strong, well-conditioned body was useless. My friends and popularity were not doing me any good. I simply did the only thing that I could do: I gave up.

The next thing I knew, I was being filled with love. It was as if Jesus joined me in that hospital bed, and all I could do was say, "I love You, Jesus; I love You, Jesus; I love You, Jesus." Over and over again, literally for hours, I repeated "I love You, Jesus," not because I was trying to get something from Him, but because I had already received something from Him. He gave me life! He allowed me to slip within a breath of death, so that I would know that I was His and not my own.

At that point I got radically better. All pain was gone. I was miraculously healed. Even the doctors admitted they did nothing to cure me and that it was indeed God who healed me. I had lost fifty pounds during that week, but I would regain my strength. I was thrilled just to be alive. Within days I built up my hope of finishing the football season. I was a jock, and my blood pumped activity. Convalescing was killing me.

One day my doctor came in with news I could tell he was excited about. "Everything looks fine; it looks as if you'll make it without any lasting damages." I was glad.

"When can I play football again?" I eagerly asked.

"Oh," he stated coldly, "you'll never play football again."

When I heard that, something inside me died. For the first time in my life I felt bitterness and hatred. God had spared my life all right, but He killed that which I loved more than anything: football. It was dead and with it all other sports. My identity and popularity were built around sports, and in a big way I felt as though I had not survived the concussion. My security system was destroyed.

For months I carried resentment in my heart. I quickly learned not to express it, because all my well-meaning friends would hand me gum balls and say, "Oh, you can't feel like that. If it wasn't for God, you could be dead." Or, "Football isn't everything!" I knew that was true, but I still hurt because my image of who I was and my value system of what I was worth were so built around sports that it was killing me to lose it all. I was an athlete, but now that I could no longer be involved in athletics, I didn't know who I was.

Poems

One day, while still struggling over losing football, God taught me something through a very good friend who read Ephesians 2:10 (RSV) to me: "For we are his workmanship, created in Christ Jesus for good works, which God prepared beforehand, that we should walk in them."

"Fred, the word translated 'workmanship' is the Greek word *poiema,* from which we get the word *poem.* God is making your life like a poem—a thing of beauty. You are a Christian, right?"

"You better believe it," I replied.

"Then this verse is true for you; you are being lovingly formed into a piece of artwork that will bring glory to the Artist, Jesus. You might look different from what you want to look like." I nodded.

"Listen to this," he said, reading me another verse. " 'Does a clay pot dare argue with its maker, a pot that is like all the others? Does the clay ask the potter what he is doing? Does the pot complain that its maker has no skill?' " (Isaiah 45:9 TEV)

I knew that I was guilty of questioning my Potter. I was not appreciating His creativity in my life. I wanted my vessel to look one way, and He was making me another.

He read me one other verse that brought the whole thing together for me. " 'Do not look on his appearance or on the height of his stature, because I have rejected him; for the Lord sees not as man sees; man looks on the outward appearance, but the Lord looks on the heart' " (1 Samuel 16:7 RSV).

I had been measuring the value of my life according to what I did outwardly—my athletic accomplishments. I enjoyed them because my friends would recognize them, and they thereby affirmed my worth. When my sports were gone, I thought I was worthless, but I was wrong.

My friend and I prayed. I asked Jesus to forgive me for my ungratefulness, and I actually thanked Him for taking sports out of my life. I told Him to continue His artwork. That day God taught me to respect myself, not because of my own abilities, but because of what He was making me.

Lasting Security

Jesus so wants us to be secure that He tells us to find our security in Him. After all, we have seen that insecurity is "building our lives around that which can be taken away from us," so in order to be secure, we must build our lives around that which cannot be taken from us: God. He wants us to find our security in Him: in the facts that He originally made us; that He died for us, expressing the greatest form of love and acceptance; and that He is remaking us to show forth His creativity.

Jesus so wants us to be secure that He forbids us to find our security anywhere else. He says, "If any one comes to me and does not hate his own father and mother and wife and children and brothers and sisters, yes, and even his own life, he cannot be my disciple" (Luke 14:26 RSV). Jesus is not advocating aggressive hatred of family members, rather He is emphasizing the radical love for Himself. When Jesus calls His disciples to "hate" them, He is telling them not to find their security in family, but rather to find their security in Him. Again He says, "So therefore, whoever of you does not renounce all that he has cannot be my disciple" (Luke 14:33 RSV).

Jesus emphasized that temporal beauty, skills, or relationships will never give lasting security. Paul found his identity in Jesus, for he was able to say, "For me to live is Christ . . ." (Philippians 1:21).

- The jock says, "For me to live is sports."
- Body beautiful says, "For me to live is a beach."
- The businessman says, "For me to live is money."
- The drug freak says, "For me to live is freebase."
- The student says, "For me to live is the honor roll."
- The Christian says, "For me to live is Christ."
- What do *you* say?

1. What would you change about yourself if you were able?
2. Do you think you're "cool"? Why or why not?
3. Even though Jesus says, "Come as you are," why is that sometimes hard?
4. The author was deeply hurt when he lost football. What have you ever lost that was close to you?
5. Where can our lasting security be found? Why?

1. When you meet new people, by what criteria do you judge them?
2. Why are so many people concerned about what "the group" thinks of them?
3. How would you define *insecurity?* What makes people feel insecure?
4. Is it wrong to love yourself?

3 The Faltering Family

The family is faltering. The one place that was intended to provide a haven of rest has become a holocaust. That which promises to be a foxhole has become the center of the battleground. Every year more and more young people face family failure. When they cry out, "Anybody home?" they do not get an answer.

One night during high school I was out late with my friends. I made sure that I drove into our driveway very slowly and quietly, so as not to wake up my parents. To my surprise, all the lights in the house were on. And just my luck, I had forgotten to bring my house key along. Very sheepishly I knocked on the door. When no one answered, I rang the bell. I began to get concerned at that point and knocked more loudly. Finally I began to yell, "Anybody home?" trying in vain to get their attention. "*Anybody home?*" No answer. At this point my mind ran wild, imagining all sorts of hideous things that might have happened to them. *Where could they be? Did someone break in on them and. . . ?* With no further options available to me, I went around to the side of the house, lowered my shoulder to the door, and blasted my way into the house, tearing the door off the hinges and destroying the latch. "*Anybody home?*" I screamed. Again no answer. I ran pantingly from room to room, downstairs first and then upstairs. No one was there. "Where could they be?" I asked myself out loud. Within moments, headlights came down the driveway. I knew at once it was the rumble of my parents' car. I breathed a huge sigh of relief. Although to this day I do not think they understood why I tore the door off the hinges, for those moments when I was convinced that my parents might have been in trouble, nothing mattered to me as much as their safety. When they came into the house, I was so relieved they were home that I did something I never did any other time as a teenager: I actually threw my arms around them and wept.

That was an unusual experience for me, but there are teenagers all over the world who have at least a taste of those feelings of insecurity and loss every single night. For many, their parents are never home. For others their parents might be home, but they do not care. In either case there is a deep sense of loss. There is an obvious emptiness that eats at them like a hunger pain. Every one of us who has been in a faltering family has felt cheated.

Better Homes & Gardens ran a nationwide survey of 300,000 people. They made some remarkable discoveries. When asked, "Do you feel that family life in America is in trouble?" 76 percent answered, "Yes." When asked, "Do you feel happier at home than anywhere else?" an overwhelming 85 percent answered positively.

These statistics make my heart heavy, because they show that essentially we all know the family is in bad shape, yet we still look to it for our security. For teenagers this means piles of insecurity.

Divorce

For a kid to go to bed at night hearing his parents screaming at each other or talking about a divorce is like trying to sleep through an earthquake: The foundation is cracking, the walls crumbling, and the roof is about to fall. Divorce and separation always hurt. Any normal young person whimpers the insecure cry, "What is going to happen to me?" and the question is often pathetically answered, "Ah, I guess it doesn't really matter anyway!"

This is what a teenager from Boston has said: "I was never anything to my mother but another kid to feed and throw away.... Then when she thought I was big enough, she told me to get out and not come back. I was thirteen."

Every year there are 2 million marriages. That is fine. But every single year there are 1 million legal divorces. That is pitiful. Sociologists estimate that there are an additional 1 million unofficial poor-man divorces. That is devastating. It means for every marriage there is a disaster, and for kids that means a pile of pain. All over the country there are teens who long to live with mom and dad. The problem is that mom and dad do not want to live with each other. Acquiring legal custody of a child often degenerates into a bitter battle resembling two dogs tearing a towel in opposite directions. The cry goes up, "Hey, what about me? What is going to happen to me?"

Dr. Jack Westman, psychiatrist at the University of Wisconsin, is heavily involved in divorce counseling. He states, "Most parents going through divorce aren't aware of how it's affecting the kids." He said that young people have suffered under the family collapse in various ways: anywhere from bed-wetting and thumb-sucking; to poor grades in school; to alcohol, drugs, and sex. There are many visible scars caused by the underlying problem: the faltering family.

Abuse

I met Sally in Chicago. Her parents were separated before she was a teenager. Her father was an alcoholic, and her mother was a practicing witch and lesbian. Sally spent her first night out on the street when she was eleven, sleeping in a garbage can. She faced all the same struggles every other high-school student faced, but without the support of the loving arms of a mother or the strong shoulders of a father. She had nowhere to go and no one to tell her that she was normal.

Sally knew what it was to be abused by her parents. She had been stabbed, had chairs broken over her head, and had the scars to prove it. For Sally and the thousands of kids like her, it is probably impossible to describe the hopelessness such mistreatment caused, especially since it came from those who were supposed to *love* her.

Hardly a week goes by in which some hideous expression of child abuse does not appear in the newspaper. Every time I read one such article, the question pops into my brain, *Whatever happened to love?*

Sociologist Richard Gelles states, "Our study has discovered a violent generation under thirty years of age." He shows that parents under thirty are five times as violent as older parents.

I question, *What is going to happen to kids over the next ten years?* The answer comes back loud and horrifyingly, *They'll suffer even more pain!*

Neglect

For every kid who suffers under active abuse, there are dozens who suffer under passive abuse. There are kids all over the world who are fully convinced that they are less important to their parents than the TV set or the evening newspaper. Yet those parents who mistreat their kids with neglect scratch their heads when their daughter gets pregnant in the arms of some misfit who took time to show her at least thirty minutes of affection.

In the 1960s families across America were being threatened by teenagers running away from home. Every major newspaper and magazine carried articles on the runaways. Billboards throughout the country were being rented by parents who pleaded with their daughters to come home. We no longer read as much newsprint on the subject, but the disease is still there—in fact it is stronger than ever. Every year between .5 million and 2 million American youth run away; the conservative side of that estimate would indicate an average of nearly 10,000 teens every week are trying to escape. The problem is still with us, but according to *U.S. News & World Report,* officials are now diagnosing the statistics differently: Instead of runaways, these persons are now seen as "throwaways." The Office of Youth Development of the Department of Health and Human Services, formerly the Department of Health, Education, and Welfare, suggests that approximately 28 percent of the runaways have been forced out of their homes. It is the parents who run away; they are running away from their responsibilities.

When I met Peter, he was in a rehabilitation center. He had grown up in a nominally Christian home, but he hated his father. I will let him tell the story: "When I was younger, my dad was always gone. He had two jobs and wanted to make a bundle of money. When he was home, he would always put me down. I was afraid to have friends visit me, because he made me feel like such a jerk in front of them. I could never do enough to please him, no matter how hard I tried. He was hardly ever around. I wouldn't see him for days. I'd do anything for attention. The only way I'd see him was if he had to come pick me up at school after detention. When things got worse with me, he got stricter. He was hardly ever around, but when he was, he'd let me have it, to make up for the time when he wasn't there. I started to hate authority—all authority. When my parents didn't know what to do with me anymore, they put me in this rehabilitation center for delinquent kids. At least it got me out of the house, and they didn't have to deal with me anymore."

The basic problem Peter faced was not abuse; it was neglect. Peter longed to be treated like a person. He had feelings he wanted his dad to know about, but those feelings just sat there like a stack of unread newspapers. Inside Peter was hungry for affection, but there was no one to give it to him.

I suppose whether kids drop out or get thrown out really does not matter. In either case the situation must be hideously wrong for a kid to leave. The street provides little warmth for anyone. You do not get affection from asphalt. We wonder why the teenage crime rate is so high: According to *Seventeen* magazine, one-half of all the people arrested are between the ages of ten to twenty, while that is only one-fifth of the country's population. Some say this is due to lax laws or a crummy penal system. These might add to the problem, but I hear kids saying something different, "Why not break the law? I'd just as soon spend time in jail. It's no worse than home."

Couples are parenting children as if they were animals. When children are young, they are entertaining, like kittens; but when they become full-grown cats, they get thrown away. Many of the teenagers that fill the streets of our cities are one-time house cats who have become alley cats because their parents' love grew cold. Ten thousand a week means that there are a pile of hurting kids.

Where Do You Go?

When a kid leaves home or when his home falls apart, where is he or she supposed to go? If these teenagers cannot turn to their homes or if they have no place to call home, then they will answer this question, *"No place!"* The expression "There's no place like home" has never been as well understood as it has by teenagers in the 80s. In fact many young people do not know what home is, period.

When Sally, my friend in Chicago, realized that her home was shattered, she climbed into a garbage can for the night. Every kid who has lost his home has reached for some sort of garbage can. Some reach for their earphones and try to lose themselves in the bombardment of stereophonic sounds. Others find books to be good tranquilizers.

Parents all over the world have pulled their hair out over the past two decades, saying, "What has happened to the kids today? Why, I would never have thought of doing these things!" Has the world changed? Yes, to some extent it has. However I would say the real problem is not that kids are exposed to more garbage than ever before. The big difference is that today the family is not providing the support system it used to, enabling the teens to weather the storms they face. And because the family is faltering and failing, kids are forced to look elsewhere for relief.

A very sensitive blind musician, Ken Medema, puts it this way:

> If this is not a place
> Where tears are understood
> Then where shall I go to cry?
> And if this is not a place
> Where my spirit can take wings
> Then where shall I go to fly?
>
> I don't need another place
> For tryin' to impress you
> With just how good and virtuous I am,

No, no, no
I don't need another place
For always bein' on top of things
Everybody knows that it's a sham,
It's a sham
I don't need another place
For always wearin' smiles
Even when it's not the way I feel
I don't need another place
To mouth the same old platitudes
Everybody knows that it's not real

So if this is not the place
Where my questions can be asked
Then where shall I go to seek?
And if this is not the place
Where my heart cry can be heard
Where, tell me where,
Shall I go to speak?

So if this is not the place
Where tears are understood
Where shall I go, where shall
I go to fly?

When the home feels like hell, teenagers are stuck like flies in a furnace: They are sure to get burned. The fragile emotions of adolescence are not equipped to service the red-hot experiences they face without a father and mother to help them. At times parents need to act as shock absorbers, Band-Aids, security blankets, road signs, and punching bags. But when the parents are not there or do not care, the teenagers are left to fry.

4 Parental Pain-Relievers

I do not care how dynamite your parents are; it is almost impossible to make it through adolescence without having at least a minor dose of parental pain. The minute you start making decisions on your own—what Santa Claus will bring you for Christmas, what flavor ice-cream cone you want, or what to name your pet frog—is when conflicts begin between you and your parents.

Being a baby means that your parents are fully responsible for your actions. When you are first born, all the decisions are made for you: what flavor baby food you eat, what color socks you wear, when you lie down or sit up, how many kisses you get or give away.

Leaving childhood, you move toward adulthood. Being an adult means that *you* are fully responsible for your actions. When you get a speeding ticket, you pay the fine. When you go out to McDonald's, you pick up the tab. When you go to bed at night, you have to set the alarm.

Being a teenager is the weird stage of "betweenity": between wanting to make all the decisions, but not wanting to pay all the bills; between wanting to stay out as late as you can, but not being able to get up when you have to in the morning; between never wanting your parents to tell you what to do and wanting, more than anything in the world, to have them tell you they are interested in everything that you do.

Responsibility Transfer

The transfer of responsibility from the parents to the teenager is rarely done as graciously as the passing of the baton in a mile relay. Sprinters who run in relays practice for hours on how to release the baton and how to receive it without breaking stride. It does not come easily, even with a little aluminum pipe. It should not surprise us then that passing the baton of life takes even more time and causes considerable heartache. "Who has the baton?" is a major question in the home. There are times when nobody knows who has it, and there are times when everyone wants it. Either way, people are going to get hurt.

We have a preconceived notion that responsibility transfer automatically happens between the ages of twelve and twenty-one and that during those years a person needs to take on more responsibility, because on his twenty-first birthday, he is going to be on his own. Twenty-one is the age at which, no matter what state you are in, you can legally drink, drive, join the army, and make all your own decisions. (In many states seventeen, or even younger, is the magic age.)

While the state authorizes a certain age, the Bible does not. The laws of our country are legal and cold. God's method is far more loving and personal. Rather than an age automatically declaring you legally fit to handle areas of responsibility, God, who knows everything about us—all our weaknesses and strengths—teaches us how to handle responsibility, through our parents.

Jesus said, "No one can serve two masters; for either he will hate the one and love the other, or he will be devoted to the one and despise the other . . ." (Matthew 6:24 RSV). If this is the case, how is any teenager expected to grow up without a serious conflict within his own home, where there are, in a sense, two masters?

He isn't! No one is supposed to grow up in a home where there are two masters. Trying to live under such dual authority is never healthy and will always lead to problems and pain.

"But I Can't Obey Them, I Hate Them"

When Peter's parents turned him over to the rehabilitation center with other delinquent kids, he hated it. He hated his parents for doing that to him. If anyone had told him that when he got out, he would have to obey his parents, he would have told him to stick it in his ear.

As I walked through the front door to visit Pete, the guard greeted me and pointed to his room. Pete was just coming upstairs from lunch, so I followed him outside to a bench where we sat and talked for a while. That afternoon Pete told me about all the hostility in his heart toward his father. His mother was fine, but he could not handle his dad. When he did well in school, it was never good enough. When he played basketball, he never scored enough. The only attention he got was harsh criticism. What made things worse was that his dad was gone most of the time, working two or three jobs. Since his father always paid attention to what he did wrong, Peter decided to give his dad something to really pay attention to. His morals started slipping, along with his grades. His friends changed, and so did his personality. Finally when his parents thought they had totally lost control, they saw no other option than to put someone else in charge.

We did not talk for long that day, but Peter, in expressing all his bitterness and resentment, spoke about forgiveness: "I know I need to forgive them. It hurt when he hit me and when he wouldn't visit me and when he would never admit that he was wrong, but I need to forgive them. If God can forgive me for what I did to them, I can forgive them."

I had not mentioned a word to Pete about forgiving his father. In fact we were talking about what following Jesus means, and the first thing he knew it meant was that he had to forgive his dad.

He continued, "The hardest thing is that when we met together with my counselor I admitted what I did wrong, but he never admitted doing anything. It sure would be easier to forgive him if he would admit he was wrong." I sat there and nodded in agreement. Then very quietly he added, "But I think God will help me do it anyway."

The next week I got a letter from his counselor. She could not believe the difference in his attitude. "Pete has changed. There is a definite difference in him. He is happy, and he counsels with the other guys on the floor. He has even been an encouragement to me."

I next heard that Pete was living at home with his parents and actually enjoying himself. Just yesterday I talked with him on the phone. "I still have my problems and get in disagreements now and then, but basically things are great. It was amazing, but when I submitted to my dad and let him know that I was looking to him for direction, he really started paying attention to me."

Never once since Pete has forgiven his parents have I heard him criticize his father. He not only laid down all the old weapons he used against his dad, but he actually got rid of them. Whenever he mentions the conflicts, he speaks about "my temper" or "my pride" or "my problem."

"Honoring is the hard part. That has to do with the attitude," he admits. "It's easy to obey, that's just the outward action. At times I still have to deal with resentment, but I've only gotten in one argument since I've been home. It made me feel terrible. I went to him immediately; I told him that I was wrong. I couldn't stand the division."

Peter's heart is changed. Peter knows that his father's will is in God's hands and that God will use his father to build godly character in him. He went from hating his dad to honoring him, because he was able to forgive him.

If your parents have personally assaulted you, causing you deep pain, then you will never be able to obey or honor them until you first forgive them. I know it is hard to forgive your parents, especially when they will not admit that they were wrong or when they continue to inflict similar pain. If your parents treated you like a stray dog during the divorce or if they show you very little affection, your heart might be filled with resentment. For you, that resentment is actually a bigger problem than your parents. God will handle your parents if you first let Him handle your resentment.

The problems that exist between you and your mom and dad might be 90 percent their fault and only 10 percent yours. However you need to plead guilty to your 10 percent and forgive them for the rest. Then you will be able to communicate with them, and God will be able to change them.

"But You Don't Know My Parents!"

I was reading out loud to a group of teenagers, " 'Honor your father and mother' (this is the first commandment with a promise), 'that it may be well with you and that you may live long on the earth' " (Ephesians 6:2, 3 RSV), and a girl burst out, "Yeah, that's fine for some people, but you don't know my parents." Needless to say the entire group cracked up. They laughed not only because she interrupted my reading, but because they could identify with her objection. After all, how can you honor your greatest source of irritation?

To tell some kids to honor their parents is like telling a cat to love a dog. How can you love someone who keeps chasing you and your friends up a tree?

If your father has smelly feet, a lousy sense of humor (or none at all), outdated clothing, and is famous for snoring through TV, he might be hard for you to respect. If your mother never pays any attention to you, except to instruct you to clean the table, clean up your room, or do your homework, she might be even harder to respect. You might conclude that your parents are an exception to the rule: the ones who do not deserve to be honored. If your dad has broken a chair over your head or hit you in the chops with his bare knuckles, you might feel hostility toward him. But I have news for you; no teenager was ever asked to honor a personality, but every teenager is asked to honor a position.

A parent does not win honor from a child because of a dynamic personality. A parent deserves honor simply because of the child's humble position.

There is an ugly occurrence in families across our world: Parents are rejecting children because they are not what they wanted; either they are male and they wanted female, or they are too dumb, or they were born with red hair instead of blond. It is equally ugly to think that young people would reject parents because they do not measure up to their standards.

God has this to say to all who question their parents' authority:

> Woe to him who says to his father, "What have you begotten?" or to his mother, "What have you brought to birth?"
>
> Isaiah 45:10 NIV

I pray that God will give you the grace to forgive your mom and dad if you have any bitterness in your heart against them, even as He gave that grace to Pete.

Shock Absorbers and Listeners

When a teenager has a healthy relationship with his parents, the many crises of adolescence will still be there, but at least they will be easier to understand. To get along well with your parents does not require that they have all the answers, but that you are honest enough to admit that you have some questions; it does not mean that you will always agree, but that you will respect each other when you disagree; it does not mean that you will like what they tell you, but that you will obey them anyway, with a smile.

A happy home recognizes that there is only one Master—the Lord Jesus—and everyone looks to Him for advice. Those of you who are still single look for Jesus to lead you through your parents. Even if they do not act like Christians, they can still provide protection from growing pains of life, like shock absorbers, as you ride down many rocky roads.

I want to challenge you: Sit down with your parents (you might even take them out to dinner and then sit down with them) and tell them which rules you do not like and tell them why; tell them what you would like them to do differently; then ask them to (gently) tell you everything about your behavior and attitudes that they do not like; ask them what you could do to overcome these problem areas and ask them to pray for you in these areas; and before you are done, ask them to be honest enough to tell you what they see as your greatest area of potential.

I knew Jane during her last three years of high school. She had a very tight relationship with her parents. They did not always see eye to eye, but they always talked about it. Their evening meal would often last three hours as they talked through problems. On her birthday Jane's father would buy her a corsage and take her out to dinner, just the two of them. When she was sixteen, they drove to New York City together to see a show and spend the night in a fancy hotel. I cannot think of a girl who got into more heated discussions (arguments) with her parents and yet who had a better relationship with them than Jane.

Nine times out of nine, talking will not get us into trouble, even when we do not agree. The trouble starts when the talking stops. When you stop talking, you stop trying; and when you stop trying, you start dying. *Do not* let your family die. If you have turned your room into a foxhole, barricaded with machine guns and mortars, stick a handkerchief on a bayonet and call a truce. Put down your artillery, climb out, and start talking. You will probably find out that your parents are not as weird as you thought.

What Parents?

There are some who will read these pages through tears, because they have no parents. If this is not true of you, then I am sure you have such friends. Pathetically, many wish they had parents to whom they could submit.

I was asked to speak to a group of thirty kids in the basement of a nearby home. As I climbed down the stairs, trying to avoid stepping on any teenage bodies, I was struck by one girl who stood out as being the most vibrant and full of life. Several others looked as if they had marinated in embalming fluid. Others looked as if they had just wakened, and still others looked as if they were asleep. But it was obvious that this one girl was glad she was there. When we sang, she was one of the few who clapped. When we asked who would lead in prayer, she volunteered. When I told the group how I met Jesus, some of them were tickling one another, some were trying to spear the goldfish with a Bic pen, but this girl smiled back at me as if I was telling her a story she loved to hear.

After the meeting was over, I asked someone who she was, and he said, "Oh, she has only been coming for a few weeks." (I could tell that she must have been new, because she had not picked up the apathy of the rest of the group.) Then he told me what I was most interested in, "Her parents are divorced. She is a foster child."

Time and time again as I have worked with young people I have seen that teenagers from broken homes have an added capacity to draw near to their Father in heaven.

Obviously this does not mean that it is preferable for your parents to have a divorce. However what it does mean is that when the human parents falter, your heavenly Father comes on strong.

This is why it says in the prophecy of Jeremiah that when the human leadership in the home fails, God will personally assist:

> Leave your fatherless children, I will keep them alive; and let your widows trust in me.
>
> Jeremiah 49:11 RSV

Again this same truth is communicated in the Psalms, where it calls God "Father of the fatherless and protector of widows is God in his holy habitation" (Psalms 68:5 RSV). Widows have lost their human protectors and providers: their husbands; many teenagers have lost their human protectors and providers in their fathers. In either case God provides an increased capacity for their hearts to respond to God's mercy and compassion.

Even in the case of a home where one or both parents are gone, there is still only one Master: God. When the parents are present, God is the Master through them. When they are missing, God is the Master directly.

1. What was the most disappointing experience you have ever had with your parents?
2. Have you ever felt like leaving home? Why?
3. When you're together, who does more of the talking, you or your parents?

1. List six qualities kids most want to see in their parents.
2. List six qualities parents most want to see in their children.
3. In your own words, define "betweenity."
4. What is a teenager's responsibility toward his parents? Discuss the difference between *obey* and *honor.* Why is it so hard?

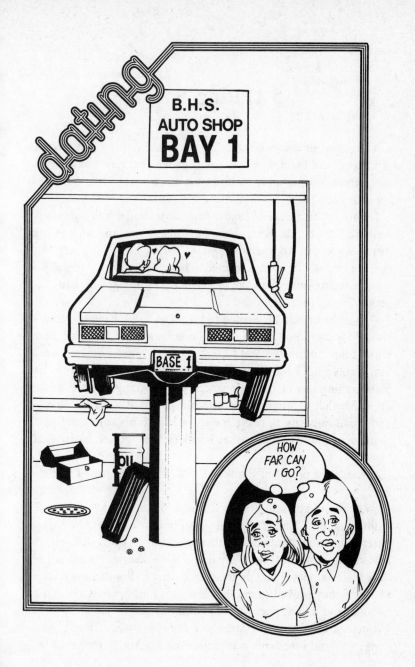

5 Dating Pains

You show me someone who has never cried over a boyfriend or girl friend, and I will show you someone who has never dated. (And that person has probably wasted even more tears.) Even hard guys get hurt dating.

Frank was my image of a hard guy. His muscular body must have weighed 220 pounds. He was good at most sports, and whenever he drove up to our youth meetings in his bright yellow Jeep with chrome "mags," he always seemed to have a new female friend who was more attractive than the last. If anyone thought he had it together, it was Frank.

One night he said he wanted to take a walk after the meeting, so we did. We had not gotten even two houses down the road, and I noticed how strangely silent he had become. When I looked over at him, I could not believe my eyes, or I should say *his eyes;* they had tears coming out of them. It struck me so strange that I did not know whether to laugh or cry with him. I had allowed his physical and social maturity to make me so callous to his emotional needs that it seemed out of place to see Frank cry. He seemed incapable of tears.

"What's the problem, Frank?" I thought perhaps I had offended him.

"You're not going to believe it," he told me. "I really feel stupid telling you this." I nodded on the basis of how awkward he looked. After some more apologies he finally told me, "I love Liz, but she tells me she just wants to be my friend." He was right; I did not believe it—or at least I had difficulty believing it. But those tears were real, and they proved to me that his heart hurt because the girl he had spent so much time with now wanted out.

I do not care who you are, there are times when dating seems dangerous and threatening. It turns even mighty, macho men into insecure mice. Larry Norman, a very long-haired and tender-hearted musician sings about breaking up in "I've Got to Learn to Live Without You." In it he describes the up-and-down dynamics of dating:

You came into my life, you took me off the shelf
You told my name to me and taught me what to do
But then you went away and left me by myself
I feel completely lost and lonely without you.

Why'd you go baby
I guess you know
I've got to learn to live without you

Today I thought I saw you walking down the street
With someone else I turned my head and faced the wall
I started crying and my heart fell to my feet
But when I looked again it wasn't you at all.

It is so easy to build our lives around "my girl" or "my boy." We love what we see in these people, and we love who we are when we are with them. They become mirrors that let us see only the best things about ourselves, while covering up the blemishes. As long as they are there the feelings of affection at least bounce off them, back at ourselves; and we feel great, especially about ourselves. But when we break up, our foundation is gone; the mirror is shattered; and our heart's affections are lost in space. We hurt because we still love, but we are not loved in return.

Why the Pain?

Dating is a lot of fun, but it has caused teenagers to cry a reservoir of tears. Some cry because of breaking up with the ones they thought loved them. Some tears are caused by sitting home weekend after weekend when everyone else gets asked out. The reason why dating causes so much pain is because it is usually done wrong. After all, there is no time to practice. By the time you are into junior- or senior-high school, you are thrown into the pool of dating and are expected to know how to swim. Because they do not teach "Dating" in most high schools, most of us have to learn by trial and error, and unfortunately we spend most of our time doing it wrong.

The Overcommitted Relationship.   Have you ever told anyone that you loved him or her? Have you ever kissed someone on the first date? Have you ever become physically involved with a person of the opposite sex? If you can answer yes to any of the above, then you have been overcommitted, and you have probably either hurt someone else or hurt yourself in the process.

Larry had been dating Glenda for only four months when he came to me in a panic, "She wants to get married!" After I calmed him down, he gave me the details. "She loves me. I mean she *really* loves me. She says she can't live without me and that she wants to spend the rest of her life with me, and I just don't know. The more she talks about the future, the faster I run for the door." He said all that on his feet. Then he flopped back in a chair as if he had just dumped a seventy-pound sack out on the floor. "What do you think?" he said, as if to say, "Now it's your problem. What are you going to do about it?"

He obviously wanted an easy answer, but I wanted him to see the source of the problem. So I asked him a very pointed question, "Are you physically involved?"

He looked at me as if he were caught stealing money from his mother's purse and stated, "We've had our problems."

Since he was already partially embarrassed, I asked him another personal question, "Have you ever told her that you loved her?"

"Yeah," he said matter-of-factly and then added apologetically, "but I haven't told her that for a long time—more when we first started dating." He did not know it, but the fact that he expressed his love for her early in their relationship made things worse.

"You have gotten yourself overcommitted, and there is no way out except for either or both of you to get hurt." I explained what I meant. "You told her that you loved her when you were first getting to know her, even before you knew her well enough to accurately say those words. All you meant was, 'What I know about you is appealing,' but what she heard you say was, 'I deeply respect everything about you, and I commit myself to you exclusively.' Those three words, *I love you*, mean more to a girl than we sometimes realize. In fact guys will often use those words for their own lustful and selfish desires, to simply get girls to give themselves to them physically. But regardless of whether or not those three words were used to get her to give herself to you physically, you did become physically involved. Your sexual involvement has further communicated your commitment to her. When she consented to develop a physical relationship with you, she was sure that there was no turning back. She was playing for keeps."

He never took his eyes off of me the whole time I was talking. When I was done, he ran into his room and brought out a letter he had just gotten from her. In it he read, "Larry, the other night we did something together that I never wanted to do until I was married." The connection was obvious. Larry started to understand that Glenda combined the word *love* and the activities of sex and took it for granted that there would be a permanent bond of marriage.

Larry hung his head and begged, "So what do I do?" He had seen that the problem which developed was his fault, that he had led Glenda to expect more from him than he had any intention of fulfilling. He assured me that he did not love her enough to make a commitment to her, and he realized that he should never again carelessly use the word *love*. He also realized the sinfulness of his ways. "The only fair thing that you can do is, having recognized all the pain you have caused her, to go to her and ask her forgiveness. Chances are by now she realizes that your feelings have not been honestly communicated anyway. The truth often hurts, but it never hurts as much as extended lies."

It is so easy to take the Nestea plunge into a relationship without giving it much thought; before you know it, you are up to your arm-pits in quicksand. During our teenage years we specialize at quick, disposable relationships. But the expression "Easy come, easy go" is a can of kitty litter! A romance might come easily, but it goes very slowly and painfully. We need to be responsible for the progress a relationship makes, being careful that we do not allow our emotions to mislead us.

The Underconcerned Relationship.   Have you ever sat making out (kissing) for an extended period of time while your mind was miles away? Have you ever treated a boyfriend like a disposable can, draining the contents and tossing him in the gutter? Dating often degenerates into such an ego trip that people are used and abused as if they were made out of aluminum.

I got a friend a blind date with a very good-looking cheerleader. I thought to myself, *Wow, wait until he sees her. He won't believe it!* Everything was set: We got a huge watermelon and met at the lake to go swimming. We had a great time together. The girl was ob-viously enjoying my friend as we swam a half mile out to a raft in the middle of the lake, pushing the watermelon along. When we got to the raft, he carried the watermelon up the slide and dropped it onto the raft, breaking it in a hundred pieces. We ate it until I thought we would sink. We played water tag around the float and then went out for burgers.

The next thing I knew, they were seeing a lot of each other. She liked the fact that he was a star football player, and he liked her. He was spending all kinds of money on her, taking her to movies, buy-ing her little gifts, and taking her out to dinner. Then the money started to run out. When football season was over, she started mak-ing up all sorts of excuses why she could not see him on weekends. One night my friend and I were standing in line at a Dairy Queen and guess who stepped out of a bright red new Firebird? Yup! His girl friend. And you know who was driving it? The center for the basketball team.

Well, you can be sure that my friend called her up and had a few choice things to say to her. All she could say to him was, "I'm sorry. I had a lot of fun with you, and you are a great guy, but now I found someone better."

Needless to say, he felt used. He had spent his money, and now that his money was gone, so was his girl friend. During football season, he was a hot item, but now that basketball season was here, she wanted someone who was still in the spotlight. The ugly part was that she did not even care; she was underconcerned.

The reason teenagers often get burned dating is because they are taken advantage of—used and abused. When a girl goes out with a guy because of his money or looks or popularity, or when a guy goes out with a girl because she gives him sex, there is something desperately wrong. The relationship is based on "what *I* get" instead of "who *you* are." The I-centered friendship will always be lopsided and will rarely last very long. When we seek to please ourselves, we will be insensitive to others, and they will consistently get hurt.

The Ingrown Relationship.   One of the most common problems that develops between a boy- and girl friend is that they become ingrown. Other relationships and other activities get choked out, because they spend all their time together. This is always an unhealthy situation, but it is almost impossible to tell that to a couple when they think they are in love. Such love is more like infatuation.

Sarah's parents were scared, so they called for help. They had been encouraging Sarah to develop a social life for years, but she always felt too ugly. She would frequently get asked out on dates, but she would never accept. For some reason, the night we had a party in her barn, she started hanging around with one of the boys. That next day he came to her house, and they rode horses together. Then they went swimming together. At night they spent hours on the phone. At first, her parents were thrilled about it. *Finally, she has a social life, and she does something besides read and groom her horses,* they thought. But now that Sarah knew what it was like to have someone love her, she was overwhelmed. No one taught her how to handle the emotional whirlwind of love. She was being swept away. Her horses had not been groomed in a month. Her schoolwork was suffering severely. She never saw her parents anymore. She even stopped attending church services with her parents. When she went, she went with her boyfriend. When her parents suggested taking a vacation without him, Sarah flew into a rage: "Me go with you without him? You've got to be kidding! We are in love, and I couldn't live for two weeks without him."

We are all familiar with "puppy love." Anyone who experiences such emotional infatuation is confident that what he feels is the real thing. It is impossible to tell him anything different. Parents have gone gray trying.

If you are in the middle of an ingrown relationship, you probably hate me for saying all these disgusting things about you. If you are not, please store up this information for further reference, so you do not allow yourself to get lost in an emotional fogbank.

The Overpossessive Relationship. Frequently when a close relationship develops between teenagers, particularly younger teens, they tend to be overpossessive. At an age when our personal identities are being formed and when kids are asking, "Hey, am I worth anything?" a friend of the opposite sex assures us that we are of value. We can almost say to ourselves, "I like what I see in myself when I am with you, and I am willing to do whatever I need to do to keep you."

A few weeks ago I talked with Pam. We were talking about her boyfriend, and she told me that she did not know what she would do without him. Such an expression of dependence triggered an unhealthy response in me, so I asked her, "Why?"

Without hesitation she responded, "Because he makes me feel worthwhile."

I aimed right at the heart of the problem and asked, "But aren't you worthwhile without him?"

She hesitated. At first she said, "Well, yeah, but you know what I mean." I knew part of what she meant, but I was afraid that she was not aware of the other part. Within a moment she burst out in tears and said, "I've never had a friend before—no one to tell me that I am pretty and smart and fun. Even my parents have never shown me the affection that he has. He does make me feel important; at least I'm important to him."

We talked for a long time after that, and Pam realized that she was in a dangerous position in which she could easily be hurt. She was looking to her boyfriend for her source of security, and if he dropped her for someone else, she would be broken beyond repair.

I asked her one final question, "Do you ever feel jealous?" At that she laughed out loud.

"Jealous!" she exclaimed, "If he ever talks about someone else, I get furious. One time when we were at his house, the phone rang and it was another girl. I wouldn't talk to him for three days."

Pam was overpossessive because her life was being built upon this boy. She looked at any other potential girl friends the way a building looks at an earthquake. Pam guarded him with her life and was willing to do anything to keep him.

Many in overpossessive relationships protect their insecurities by "going steady." A ring, a varsity jacket, or an ID bracelet is often given as a symbol of such a commitment. It is like a sign that says, NO TRESPASSING; VIOLATORS WILL BE PROSECUTED, or, THIS ONE'S MINE, BABY, KEEP YOUR HANDS OFF! Even much of the dating terminology speaks in terms of possessiveness: *"My* boyfriend" or *"my* girl." Such expressions seem to imply a sense of ownership. This whole concept needs to be smashed, because it is the basis for the majority of the dating problems we have considered.

Why the Failure?

We have said that the reason dating causes so many tears is because it is usually done wrong. Why do so many teenagers, generation after generation, keep failing at it? (Hang on to your chair as you read the answer.)

The reason dating involves so many failures and causes so much pain is because it is usually practiced after the demonic pattern of this world, without any guidance from Jesus. Ordinarily we date the way every other kid at school dates, so we follow the pattern of this world.

Listen to the way the apostle Paul describes the ways of the world:

> In the past you were spiritually dead because of your dis-obedience and sins. At that time you followed the world's evil way; you obeyed the ruler of the spiritual powers in space, the spirit who now controls the people who disobey God.
>
> Ephesians 2:1, 2 TEV

Obviously it is not fitting for a child of God to follow the dating established by the world. Jesus does not want any of His children to fall into such pitfalls, nor does He want them to suffer the pain.

If you have dated and have been hurt, take heart! God has a better way. If you have yet to begin dating, then do not follow the patterns you see around you, but consider the following option.

6 Update

I have seen whole groups of teenagers change when they began to look critically at the old forms of dating and exchange them for a new concept of dating. This new method of dating is so radically different that the other day a friend of mine came up to me and asked, "Fred, this new way of dating is not really dating, is it?" I chuckled out loud and told him that he was catching on. In many ways it is not dating; that is, it is not the standard method of dating. We call it "update," because it is actually a step up from the traditional, worn-out, ho-hum variety that has caused so many tears through the years.

The old style of dating was based on ownership: "You are *my* girl, because *I* brought you to this party; so you have to spend the night with *me* and do whatever *I* say." Or, "You can't go out with any other girls, because you are *my* boyfriend. You took *me* to the prom, so you have to spend all your weekends with *me.*"

This old style of dating was preliminary marriage activity. Young people have asked themselves, *Is this the one? Have I found the ultimate woman?* or, *Would he be a good father to my children? Could I spend the rest of my life with him?* So many young people go through boy- or girl friends like Kleenex, because they are hunting for the ultimate mate and classify all members of the opposite sex into two categories: *marriageable* or *out of the question.*

The traditional technique of dating was often motivated by sex. It degenerated into the without-a-kiss-on-the-first-date-it's-been-a-total-waste mentality. Some guys categorize girls into two groups: Those who mess around, and those they would marry. We live in the aftermath of the sexual liberation, when very few teenagers have been able to maintain strong moral convictions. Thirty percent of teenage girls and 50 percent of teenage boys are sexually active

before the age of sixteen. The Bible described the prophets of the
sexual revolution long before they ever wagged their lying tongues:

> With their high-sounding nonsense they use the sensual pull
> of the lower passions to attract those who were just on the
> point of cutting loose from their companions in evil. They
> promise them liberty. Liberty!—when they themselves are
> bound hand and foot to utter depravity. For a man is the
> slave of whatever masters him.
>
> 2 Peter 2:18, 19 PHILLIPS

Such an attraction to members of the opposite sex has destroyed
many teenagers, and it will destroy many more. Surely dating was
never intended to provide a playground for sexual destruction.

The Lord of Dating

Even those of us who hypocritically profess to follow Jesus
should know by now that our lives are supposed to be Christ centered and not self-centered. Yes, that means that even dating is
supposed to be Jesus centered. Impossible? No! If it is impossible,
then Jesus is still in the grave.

If Jesus is Lord of your life—that is, if you are willing to do whatever He says, regardless of what it will cost you—you must realize
that He wants to be Lord of your dating life. Jesus did not say,
"Follow me, and I will make you daters of men." Nor did he say,
"Seek ye first the most beautiful girl on campus, and all these things
will be added unto you." He wants you to seek Him first and to be
more concerned about pleasing Him than going out on a Saturday
night.

If you have a special boyfriend or girl friend, can you place him
or her on God's altar, not necessarily indicating that you will never
again see each other, but that you will seek Jesus' ways before you
seek each other? Would you be willing to ask God to take this person

out of your life if He does not think you are good for each other? I am aware this might sound as if I am asking you to pluck out your eyes, but let me explain. Often the things that we are the most emotionally involved with are the things that are the most dangerous to us.

Not long ago my two-year-old son was walking through the kitchen. He reached up on the counter and grabbed a sharp carving knife by the blade. He came running into the living room, chuckling, "Look, dada! Look what I have, dada!" He thought he had a treasure, nice and shiny. I gasped! As I reached for it, his little fingers grasped the razor-sharp blade tighter, and he pulled it back, saying, "No, dada, mine!" He was right; it was his at that moment. But just because it was in his grasp and highly appealing to him, it was also highly dangerous. If I had stripped it out of his hands, I would have sliced through his tiny fingers and maimed his little hand for life. As his father I had to communicate to him to give it over to me, even though he would not understand why. Finally he gave it over, and I have since taught him the uses and abuses of knives.

In the same way, dating is very appealing to all of us. It is fun and exciting. It is also potentially dangerous. Our loving Father will not tear it from our fingers, because we, too, would get maimed. As young people we are in such a formative stage that we must be careful not to scar ourselves from improper relationships. Jesus lovingly convinces us to give that "special someone" over to Him or even to give our dating lives in general. In our hearts we must purpose to maintain close fellowship with Jesus, even when we spend time with members of the opposite sex.

Will you yield this area of your life to the Lord Jesus now? If you do, it will set you free from future heartache.

A New View

With Jesus as our Lord, we now see dating from a different perspective. When Paul wrote his young friend Timothy, he gave him some dating advice: ". . . Treat younger men as brothers . . . and younger women as sisters, with absolute purity" (1 Timothy 5:1, 2

NIV). In relating to the opposite sex, girls are to treat the guys like brothers, and the guys are to treat the girls like sisters. With God as our Father, we certainly are brothers and sisters, and He expects us to treat one another that way. Immediately we recognize that a young man is not going to own his sister, so the possessive relationship is impossible. Nor would he think of marrying his sister. He would not think of having sex with his sister. So the old musty forms of dating become outdated.

If we are going to treat one another like brothers and sisters, we have seen a few of the pains and problems that we will avoid, but it will also provide the potential for healthy, meaningful relationships.

If it sounds boring to you to date as if you were spending an evening with your brother or sister, I am not surprised. However I was fortunate enough to grow up with a sister, and we have had a very close relationship. While we did not have a perfect relationship, we did a lot of things right. When Paul says "treat younger women as sisters," I can relate.

A Brother-Sister Relationship Seeks to Benefit the Other Person. Rather than the old, possessive, self-centered relationship, when we follow God's pattern for dating, we will do whatever we can to help the maturity and development of the *other* person.

When I was three years old, before I had learned to swim, I fell out of a rowboat. My sister immediately jumped in and saved me from drowning, even though she risked her own life in the process. She did not stand there, while I was breathing water, and ask, "Now let's see, what is in this for me?" She did it because she loved me and automatically sought to protect me.

Jerry and Liz were both seniors, and they liked each other a lot. The problem was, Liz was not a Christian; since Jerry was, he knew it would not be right to date her, because she was not his sister in Jesus. He prayed for her and decided to ask her to come to church on Sunday. That morning Liz heard for the first time that Jesus was a Person whom she could know. She asked Jerry's parents, after the service, if she could come over and talk more with them, which they were more than eager to do. That week they talked, and the next week they talked, and again the following week. You can be sure Jerry was praying constantly, because he so much wanted her to accept Jesus.

One night the phone rang. It was Liz. "We've talked a lot about Jesus, and you have helped me understand a lot of things. Finally I got up enough courage and asked Jesus to come into my life. I'm so happy!" She was happy indeed, but only half as happy as Jerry. Not only had she received eternal life, but they were able to start dating, since she was now his sister.

To my surprise Jerry kept their relationship a healthy one. He did everything possible to help her grow in Jesus. Regularly they would read the Bible together. They went to youth Bible studies and got home early enough on Saturday nights to get up on time for church.

Jerry put Liz and the relationship with Jesus before his own desires. Theirs is a good example of a brother-sister relationship.

A Brother-Sister Relationship Will Endure Hard Times. One of the ugliest parts of typical dating is all the pain that is felt by young hearts. Relationships have been known to break up for the strangest reasons: not liking the smell of her perfume, his new braces, her nagging mother, or the way he kisses. However in a brother-sister relationship, pain caused by breaking up is kept to a minimum, because even though you might see less of each other, you will still be brother and sister.

My sister will always be my sister because we have the same last name: Hartley. There is nothing we did to get each other, and there is nothing we can do to get rid of each other. I never was afraid of finding out that my sister was no longer my sister.

As Christian brothers and sisters we have the same name, *Christian,* and we will always have that name. There are times when God will give you a special, more intimate relationship, but if He does, remember that He might take it away from you, at which time you will still be brother and sister.

A Brother-Sister Relationship Is Free and Outgoing. Rather than suffering the consequences of all the ingrained weirdness of secular relationships, as Christian young people, we can experience great joy and freedom because of the secure bond holding us together: Jesus. As a Christian teenager you will be able to date without fears or jealousies or insecurities.

When I was growing up, I cannot remember a time when I told my sister I loved her. I did not have to tell her, because she knew it already. Neither can I remember a time when I sat around stewing over the question, "Does she still like me?" We did not take each other for granted, but neither did we resent it when the other was out having a good time.

You can tell how healthy a boy-girl relationship is by how tightly and covetously they cling to each other. Sally was always insecure. She was a Christian, but she constantly wondered what other people thought of her. She was even afraid to date because she had been burned once and thought that she could not handle that rejection again. When she heard about how to date Christians, she got all excited about the brother-sister idea. She realized that as long as they were brother and sister they were free to enjoy themselves.

When she met Donny, they made up their minds that they would treat each other like brother and sister. They went waterskiing together, out to McDonald's, attended youth meetings, went roller-skating, and enjoyed just about every other imaginable fun activity. They avoided the physical relationship; they never told each other that they loved each other; they just treated each other with respect. As the Bible says, "Dear children, let us not love with words or tongue but with actions and in truth" (1 John 3:18, NIV).

Sally came up to me after they had been dating for a month and said, "I have never had so much fun with a guy in my life. It sure is great to be free from all the games of trying to impress each other."

Two months later Donny was dating one of Sally's best friends, whom he ended up marrying a year later, but that did not bother Sally at all. In fact Sally attended their wedding and was thrilled that they had gotten together. She had no regrets because she and

Donny were still brother and sister, and she had greatly benefited from the relationship. God taught her how to overcome the insecurities caused by secular dating and how to enjoy a boy-girl friendship.

I hope this new concept of dating has made sense to you. I am sure it sounds radical. It is radical! It is what a very traditional God has to say about a very untraditional form of dating. More than being understandable, I hope it seems livable. There are hundreds—even thousands—of teenagers who have broken loose from the outdated forms of boy-girl relationships and have found great fulfillment doing things God's way. What about you?

(If you would like to read further about God's approach to dating, read my book Update, *also published by the Fleming H. Revell Company.)*

7 "How Far Can I Go?"

Now that we have understood that there is a radical difference between the *concept* of Christian dating and secular dating, we also need to understand that there is a very definite difference between the *conduct* of Christian dating and secular dating.

There is much confusion in young Christians' brains over the question, "How far can I go?" If you consider the answer you get from your parents, you may wonder if your parents just do not want you to have any fun. If you consider the life-style of your friends at school, you probably wonder why you are even asking the question. Frequently young people enter into boy-girl relationships without having satisfactorily answered that question. They assume that kissing is fine under almost any condition (white) and that sexual intercourse is wrong (black), with all sorts of gray in between. Unfortunately that gray area has caused much heartache.

Disgustingly, scores of youth magazines are telling teenagers that God does not answer the question "How far can I go?" On an airplane I read an article in a leading secular magazine that gave me heartburn, informing girls how to appear sensual to guys. It degenerated dating into sex. Later that afternoon, I picked up a so-called Christian magazine, and I read that it is perfectly normal and acceptable to have sexual relations outside of marriage and even that masturbation (sexually arousing yourself to the point of orgasm) was nothing to be ashamed of. It is one thing for the secular community, which does not know any better, to say that, but for Christians to say it, especially to young people, made me cry.

Jesus spoke of these false teachers when He said:

> Whoever causes one of these little ones who believe in me
> to sin, it would be better for him to have a great millstone

74

> fastened round his neck and to be drowned in the depth of the sea. Woe to the world for temptations to sin! For it is necessary that temptations come, but woe to the man by whom the temptation comes!
>
> Matthew 18:6, 7 RSV

And again He said, "Whoever then relaxes one of the least of these commandments and teaches men so, shall be called least in the kingdom of heaven" (Matthew 5:19 RSV).

Regardless of what any false teachers have told you, you are not ready to start dating until you have answered the question "How far can I go?" from a biblical perspective.

More problems in dating have been caused by immorality than anything else. Almost every problem situation we looked at in the previous chapter involved physical activity. In fact in all my years of youth ministry, I have had only one person who was not somehow lustfully involved come to me with serious dating problems, and that one person might have been lying. There are certainly other problems that develop, but they are all relatively small and easily resolved if there are no moral problems.

Before you start dating or before you date anymore, be sure that you establish biblical convictions in the area of sexual activity and refuse to compromise these, regardless of what it costs you. If you plunge into dating before you do this, it will be like swimming in a pool of piranha.

God's Moral Standard

The Bible was never intended to be a family heirloom, collecting dust on your mother's end table. It is God's loving rule book for life. It includes guidelines for our faith and behavior, and it draws very straight lines. There are all sorts of lies told about God's standards of morality. It is important for us to expose some of these misconceptions.

"God Doesn't Tell Us How Far We Can Go." When I was nineteen, I met a girl who was different from all the others. I liked her a lot and wanted to make sure that I did not make any mistakes, so I went to the bookstore and bought every book they had on dating and courtship—sixteen of them! I put all but one of the books in two categories: Either they were outdated books written by older men who could not speak my language, or they were written by young, contemporary authors who refused to take a stand on anything. The one book I liked has since gone out of print. I got little help from the books. The most confusing aspect of my reading was the fact that almost everyone disagreed when it came to the area of sex. Some treated the subject as if it was an evil invention of the devil. That I could not swallow. Others said that it was natural to develop a physical relationship with a member of the opposite sex. They suggested that as you get to know each other socially, mentally, and spiritually, it was normal to experiment sexually as well. That I would not swallow either.

The Bible *does* speak clearly to the subject. The key to understanding what God's moral standards are in dating is to understand His terminology.

The first three actions of the sinful nature listed in Galatians 5:19 are sexual: "fornication, impurity, licentiousness." Of these three words, the only one most of us understand is *impurity*. Even *fornication* is misunderstood.

1. *Fornication* (*porneia* in Greek): Naturally this word includes any form of sexual intercourse outside of marriage. However you can recognize that we get the word *pornography* from the same root as the Greek *porneia*. Jesus even linked the word with looking at women lustfully (Matthew 5:28), thereby extending the sin to include acts other than out-and-out sexual intercourse.

2. *Impurity* is more clearly understood. It speaks generally of any form of moral uncleanness.

3. *Licentiousness* (*aselgeia* in Greek): In some English Bibles this word is translated "debauchery" or "lasciviousness," but no matter how it appears, it is rarely understood. It is not surprising that few teenagers know how far they can go when they do not understand what this word means. Literally translated, it means, "a sensual sense of voluptuousness" (Kittle, *Theological Dictionary of the New Testament*). Put more simply, it is to "follow the inclination to sensuality" (Bane, *Greek Lexicon*).

To put this in dating language, any activity that follows a tendency or inclination toward lust is wrong. I have yet to meet a boy or girl who can engage in even preliminary forms of petting without arousing lust. The Bible plainly states, "So flee youthful lusts." It does not say, "Mess around and get as close as you can, without going all the way."

God *does* tell us how far we can go. His standard is *no lust.* "Passion rots the bones," He says. Petting, masturbation, and even certain forms of heavy kissing are thereby eliminated.

"God Doesn't Want Us to Have Any Fun."   Young people everywhere are fully convinced that if they follow Jesus they will be miserable. They picture God as the great Killjoy in the sky. Despite this common misconception, Jesus does not want to take the joy out of life; rather He wants to take the sting out of life. He wants to keep us from painful pitfalls. To guard ourselves morally and to reserve sexual activity until marriage does not kill freedom, rather it protects it.

"Sex *Is a Dirty Word."*   There are many today who accuse those who maintain a high moral standard of having a low view of sex. They blame the Puritans for fabricating such piety. At a debate before some 2,000 students in Lubbock, Texas, an official *Playboy* philosopher attempted to make such a deceptive remark: "Our rebellion is really against Puritanism. We are not rebelling against Christianity," as if Puritanism invented sexual hang-ups when it taught the sanctity of sex.

Does a person who favors laws against stealing have a low or a high view of property? Obviously he has a high view. Does a person who favors laws against murder have a low or a high view of human life? Obviously he has a high view. In the same way does a person who has certain sex standards have a low or a high view of sex? Again he is the one who obviously has a high view. Those with loose morals are the ones with the cheap view of sex. Sex is not dirty. It is sacred. And for that reason, it must be maintained within the strictest guidelines so that it does not get crumpled up and thrown in the mud.

Marriage is the protection for sexual activity. Within marriage it is a beautiful experience; in fact it is the highest expression of love a man and a woman can know. Just listen to what the Bible says about it:

> Let your fountain be blessed, and rejoice in the wife of your youth, a lovely hind, a graceful doe. Let her affection fill you at all times with delight, be infatuated always with her love.
>
> Proverbs 5:18, 19 RSV

God intends a Christian husband and wife to enjoy super sex, and protecting the sanctity of it until marriage makes it possible.

"Puritanical *Is a Dirty Word.*"   There were numerous times when I was in high school, and even at a Christian college, when I was called "prude" for maintaining a moral standard, as if that meant I was a weirdo. I can assure you that in a day of impurity, if you are a Christian, you had better stand out as being a prude. If you do not, there is something radically wrong with you. This does not mean that you will be treated with disrespect. Actually I have found that high-school students respect individuality, and you will certainly stand out as being different.

Remember, the second word listed among the works of the flesh, in Galatians 5:18, was *impurity.* This is the opposite of puritanism. In fact the Bible says that unless we are *puritanical* or *holy* we will not enter into heaven (Hebrews 12:14).

"But if You Loved Me, You'd Have Sex." This is one of the grandest lies of all. How many young, innocent lives have been destroyed because of this malicious appeal?

Sex, even premarital sex, is often called "making love." This is unfortunate, because it seems to make sex and love synonymous when they are not. In fact before marriage, the two are opposites.

A good response to such an appeal would be to say, "If you loved me, you wouldn't want to have sex with me," or, "If you loved me, you would not say such a thing."

Love is patient (1 Corinthians 13:4). A great example of love in the Bible is Jacob, who was willing to wait at least seven years after he fell in love with Rachel before he was finally able to marry her. If he simply wanted her body, he would never have waited, and he would have shown that he did not love *her.* By waiting all those years to develop a physical relationship, he showed that he genuinely loved her for who she was and not as an instrument to gratify his sexual appetite.

The Bible plainly condemns premarital intercourse, and it warns against any other lustful activity that will appeal to sensual instincts. Jesus wants teenagers to be free. The Bible says, "You will know the truth and the truth will make you free" (John 8:32 RSV). And again, "If the Son makes you free, you will be free indeed" (John 8:36 RSV). We are told, "For freedom Christ has set us free; stand fast therefore, and do not submit again to a yoke of slavery. . . . For you were called to freedom, brethren; only do not use your freedom as an opportunity for the flesh . . ." (Galatians 5:1, 13 RSV).

Do not let the false prophets of the sexual liberation fool you. Lust is a prison house. It has handcuffed many handsome couples and stripped them of their moral strength and integrity. Adopt

God's standards as your own, and you will be free to have fun and excitement through your dating years.

Setting the Standard

Are you willing to establish God's standard as your own, no matter what it costs? Are you willing to tell God that you will stick by it, even if it means losing that "special someone"? If so, have this talk with Jesus:

Thanks for answering the question of how far I should go. I wish that I had known this sooner. Please forgive me for all the times I have fallen short of what You wanted for me. You did die on the cross to set me free from my sins, and I thank You that You can do this. Right now I do claim Your deliverance, and I purpose from this point on, to maintain a moral standard of highest purity, avoiding physical relationships until I am married, by Your grace. In Jesus' name, Amen.

1. What are some dangers of dating?
2. What is puppy love? infatuation? Why are they not healthy?
3. What does it mean to place your boyfriend or girl friend on the altar?
4. What would you do if you really loved the person you were dating and that person was begging you to go to bed?

5. According to the Bible, what specific moral standards should we establish before we date?

1. Why do we get hurt so easily dating?
2. Break up into two groups (all men in one and all women in the other). Each group is to make a list of qualities that guys look for in girls and girls look for in guys. Come back together and discuss how valid the criteria are.
3. Why does the author use the term *update?*
4. Is *virgin* a complimentary term in your high school?
5. Does a Christian have a low view or a high view of sex?

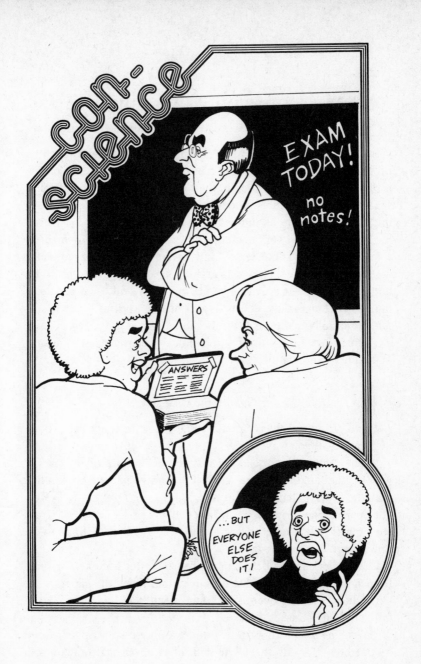

8 "My Conscience Is Killing Me"

Because we live in a scientific age in which we demand test-tube proof of anything before we are ready to swallow it, the conscience is often laughed at or hidden in the closet, like an old pair of roller skates or Beatles albums. Often, when we try to do certain things, this little guy inside us jumps up and down, waving a bright red flag, making us feel very uncomfortable. He points his big finger at something we have done wrong and screams, *"Sinner!"* Frequently we yell back at him, "Hey, who asked your opinion?" and slam the door in his face. The only problem is, that persistent voice, although muffled by our evasive efforts, is still heard. And his effect is still felt: He usually makes us feel miserable.

There are a number of ways to handle our consciences. I am sure you have tried them all. I have.

Ignore the Guy

The basic approach is to pretend that the voice is not there, hoping that it will go away.

When I entered high school, I was not much of a student. In fact when I graduated from high school I had only read one book other than the Bible. (That book was *Maybe I'll Pitch Forever,* by LeRoy "Satchel" Paige, a great black baseball player.) The school I attended was very competitive, so in order for me to pass, I had to do something.

I had never cheated before in my life, but after I flunked my first French exam, I knew I had to do something. When the papers were handed out, I looked over at my friend's paper. He got an A. "How did you do it?" I asked him.

"Easy," he said with a smile, pulling a little piece of paper from his notebook. "A crib sheet," he said. I had never heard the term. I really did not like the thought of cheating, but since he did it and since I did not like the thought of flunking French either, I made myself a cheat sheet. In fact I spent so much time inventing a fool-proof cheat sheet that I could have memorized my entire French book in less time.

Mine was perhaps the most sophisticated sheet that was ever invented. First, I went into the bookstore and bought an extra-fine-point pen to fit as much information in as little a space as possible. Then I wrote the material on a little card. I was so ignorant of French that the hardest thing was knowing what to put on the card. When the card was ready, I taped a large rubber band to the top of the card and then sewed the other end of the band into the lining of the left sleeve of my jacket. Very casually I could pull the card into my left palm with my right hand and hold it in place. Then if the teacher looked my way, I would simply release the fingers of my left hand and *presto!* it would disappear effortlessly up my sleeve and out of sight.

I perfected the use of that card for days. When the day of the exam came I walked into class with my heart beating so fast I thought the whole building was shaking. It felt as if I had a bass drum in my jacket, instead of a crib sheet. I was seated in my desk, and as the teacher walked around the room to distribute the exam he stopped at my side and stared at me. I am surprised I did not die of high blood pressure. He never said anything, but he must have thought I looked feverish. At the time all that I could think of was, *He knows what's up my sleeve.* I was frozen. Without anyone having to say a thing, I felt as if I was caught. In fact I was so guilty that I was unable to touch that card. I could not wait until I got home to take off the jacket.

Well, I flunked the test, but the humorous part of the whole story is that everyone else did, too, so the teacher was unable to count that test anyway. Actually I did not do as badly as some in the class, because by the time I had spent all that time copying and recopying the cheat sheets, I had actually learned something.

Unfortunately I did not learn enough about morals, because

when the next quiz came along, I got fearful of failing and again was tempted to cheat. I slipped the old card off the rubber band and fastened another card in its place.

I tried cheating a few more times, but later in college the Holy Spirit of God convicted me of this sin, and I repented, to never cheat again. I was even led by God to call my high-school teachers and tell them what I had done, asking them to forgive me. One teacher replied, "Oh, yes, I remember you. Well, I won't have to go back and adjust your grade, because you didn't do very well anyway."

I tried to muzzle the voice of my conscience, but it never worked. I certainly cannot say cheating does not work, even though it did not work for me. However although we might get better grades cheating, it will never help our consciences. Oh, there are times when we can continue to abuse that persistent voice, and we might even be able to muzzle it completely. However, down deep inside, there is a silent uneasiness that gnaws away and eats at us from the inside out. When we ignore its voice, it only causes problems.

Declare War

I want to tell you about a teenager who is a close friend of mine. He has been honest enough to admit to something very few even dare to think about. His name is Sam.

Sam and I were sitting in the car after a softball game and, while playing with his glove, he said to me, "I hate my conscience." I so much wished he had not said that; I did not know how to respond. Feeling my awkwardness, he said it again, "I said, 'I hate my conscience.' " He threw his glove against the dashboard and flopped back in his seat, waiting for me to say something. I did not think he needed a sermon. What he needed was a listening ear.

I knew Sam well enough to realize that he was raised in a very religious family where he was taught a strict moral standard. His parents had insisted on early curfews, short hair, and church attendance.

"I feel as if there is a tug-of-war game going on inside me," he pointed to his chest. "Why me? Why did I have to be raised in a home where they taught me that it was wrong to smoke and drink and have fun? My conscience is my worst enemy. I hate it. If only I was raised in another family, it would all be different. Why couldn't I be like every other normal kid—not a bad kid, but just able to have a little freedom. It seems that anything I do makes me feel guilty. If I go to a party and smoke a little reefer, it makes me feel unclean. All the girls are used to having sex. I don't do much, but even when I do a little, it eats me up inside. I feel as if I'm going to hell, especially on Sundays."

He talked for a long time, and I understood what he was saying. I had felt many of the same emotions. The war within his soul was pulling him back and forth. On the one hand, his conscience had a long list of do's and don'ts. His conscience kept him sitting home on weekends and getting teased by his friends on Monday mornings. Following his conscience gave him peace within himself and with his parents, but it made him lonely and bored. Sitting home and playing tiddledywinks with his kid sister was not his idea of a good time.

On the other hand, he would crumple up his conscience and throw it in the trash in order to make a few friends and avoid painful criticism. He did make friends and have some good times. But a little voice within him, which sounded a lot like his mother's, told him that God hated what he was doing. That horrible, pesty voice always ruined the good times for Sam. Every time he would go to a pot party; score with his girl friend; or guzzle a six-pack with his friends, after school, he'd feel as guilty as if he had committed murder. And in a sense he had; he was killing his conscience. The problem was, from Sam's standpoint, his conscience refused to die. He had declared war, but it would not die. That ugly, condemning finger would still point to right between his eyes and yell, "Sinner!"

After a few months of rejecting his conscience, Sam would repent and change his ways, only to get rid of the miserable guilty feeling that was driving him insane. Those first few weeks after getting "back in fellowship with God" were Sam's happiest. He would show up at every church meeting and eagerly participate in the singing and prayer. After I saw the cycle a few times, I began to recognize the glory fade. The Friday nights staying home with his kid sister wore thin. When his friends at school heard that he sang a solo in church and got baptized, they mocked him unmercifully. So, once again, seeing no other way to make friends in a secular society, he crumpled up his conscience and threw it in the trash—back where he had started.

This is a vicious circle. It is like getting stuck inside a dishwasher and living through the cycles. The only difference is that you come out feeling filthy and bruised. Declaring war on your conscience is a painful and frequently dangerous approach.

Killing the Conscience

I hope you have not reached this third level of mistreating your conscience. If you have, you have lost a friend.

Ginger and I had been friends for a long time through high school. During junior year, we started hanging around different people, since we went to different schools. I did not want to believe some of the stories I had heard about her, so I called her up, and we went out for some ice cream. After the cones were gone, she said something that struck me strangely at the time, because it was too hard to handle. "I can't cry anymore," she said.

She explained what she meant, "I used to be able to cry. When I would do something wrong, I would come home and cry about it; and when I'd pray, it would be all better. Or even in church I would cry when the preacher would talk about 'giving your life to Christ,' but I can't anymore."

Being young and not really understanding, I asked her, "Don't you feel guilty over the things you are doing?"

"No! That is just the point. I *don't* feel guilty anymore. I don't feel *anything*. After I make love with my boyfriend, it doesn't do anything to me. I can do all kinds of drugs and get drunk, but the next morning I think nothing of it. I hate feeling nothing!"

What she was telling me was that the little voice that used to accuse her when she was doing wrong was now silent. Her conscience had died because she had abused it so much.

When I drove her to her home, I felt helpless. It appeared she had lost the ability to tell right from wrong. She was like a ship without a compass—nowhere to go. I opened her door, and as she walked up the walkway she said, "But I know I will be okay. Someday when I am thirty, after I have had all my fun, I will be listening to some preacher telling about what a sinner I am, and I will cry and weep for my sins, and then I will get my life straightened out." I guess from the blank expression on my face she could tell that I was not convinced, because she said to me, "Don't you worry about me."

Well, I was concerned about her. And I am concerned about anyone in her situation, who has actually succeeded at killing his conscience, because when the conscience is dead, that built-in warning device is gone. There is nothing left to keep him from the destructive influences of evil. This girl, Ginger, has since spent time in mental institutions, has been married twice, and has less than two years to go before her thirtieth birthday. Oh, she is certainly not beyond hope; however she has suffered pathetically. Jesus loves her as much as He has ever loved her, but her life has been self-destructive, and she is reaping the fruit of her abuse.

It is interesting that the Bible says, "and keep your faith and a clear conscience. Some men [and women] have not listened to their conscience and have made ruin of their faith. Among them are Hymenaeus and Alexander . . ." (1 Timothy 1:19, 20 TEV).

Handling Guilt

The human psyche was not made to handle guilt. Bleeding ulcers, migraine headaches, hiatal hernias, and even cancer have been said to be caused by guilt. Because the inner spirit of a man rejects guilt, there are only a few options of ways to deal with it.

Change Friends.   Hanging around with goody-goodies often makes
us feel uncomfortable. I can remember when I was in seventh grade
my locker was right next to a girl I had always liked when I was
younger. But now that things were changing and I was getting into
new things to make me "cool," she stuck out as a real religious type.
She would stick little pamphlets in my locker and always acted nice
to me—almost too nice. One day, when I spilled a bottle of ink on my
gym bag, I cursed. I quickly looked over to see if she was standing
there. Her big eyes looked up at me as if she had never before heard
such filth. She did not say anything, but she didn't have to; the
message was written all over her face. Needless to say, she made me
feel terrible. Whenever I would see her coming down the hall, I
would look the other way. It was not until after I repented of sin
and cleared out my conscience that I understood why I did not like
that girl anymore. Her moral purity was offensive to my impurity.

On the other hand, we frequently make tell-me-I'm-okay relationships. Rather than simply avoiding the moral and religious
types, we hang around people who think less of religion and purity.
Often we choose to be with people who are worse than we are. They
make us feel good because we can tell that condemning voice inside
us, "Shut up! At least I'm better than they are!"

Unfortunately our consciences frequently determine our friends.
When we feel guilty around certain people, we will either straighten
up or drop out. Then we will gravitate toward the crowd that makes
us feel "at home."

Frequently parents will come to me and complain about how
their son or daughter is such a nice, loving, moral, sweet, innocent,
faithful, pure, gentle, honest, well-meaning, godly, righteous, soft-
spoken, harmless little goody-goody who is being corrupted by his
or her sinful friends. Well the Bible does say that ". . . Bad company
ruins good morals" (1 Corinthians 15:33 RSV). However I never
allow these very well-meaning but naive parents to blame other
teenagers for their own child's immoral life-style. Regardless of how
parents see their son's or daughter's heart, through their rose-
colored glasses, Jesus has said:

> For from within, out of the heart of man [or a teenager], come evil thoughts, fornication, theft, murder, adultery, coveting, wickedness,' deceit, licentiousness, envy, slander, pride, foolishness. All of these evil things come from within, and they defile a man.
>
> Mark 7:21–23 RSV

You show me a teenager who feels at home around immoral friends, and I will show you an immoral teenager. A dirty, defiled conscience feels more comfortable in the company of others who are equally or more defiled.

Rewriting the Rules. When our morals get looser, we look to new friends, not only because our old "straight" friends make us feel uncomfortable, but because the new friends agree with our new set of ethics.

If you are in this situation, can you remember back to when you thought that it was wrong to look at pornography? Perhaps you did not actually have a written rule that said, "Thou shalt not look at *Playboy* magazine," but you knew that if your mother ever found out about it, you would be in trouble. So, deep down, you thought that it was wrong. You can probably remember the first time you ever saw such a magazine. The thoughts of: *Just this once, but never again; man, if my mother ever saw me now,* overwhelmed your mind with apologies and excuses. But then the next time brought less self-condemnation and guilt, until whether officially or unofficially, you rewrote the rules to read, "Thou shalt not read *too many Playboy* magazines."

It is almost humorous, but even the most unethical people—the hardened criminals—have very strong ethics. The book and movie *The Godfather* reveal this very graphically. Killing, stealing, illicit sex, and almost every type of civil disobedience are accepted within organized crime, but only within certain perimeters. You can murder anyone you want, except on Sundays. You can go to bed with anyone, except my sister. You can steal whatever you want, as long as you put it to good use.

Some have philosophized, "Rules are made to be broken." This is a popular concept in our day of situational ethics, where many have denied the possibility of any absolute standard of right and wrong. "If there is no universal standard of right and wrong that all people will be judged by, then who is to tell me that I can't throw this brick through that window?" many have asked. "Who says I can't go to bed with my girl friend? We love each other." "Yeah, I know that drugs might be bad for my health, but my parents overeat, even though they both have high blood pressure. Everybody's going to die of something!"

When we were born, we each had a certain amount of innocence and naiveté that would accept the moral standards of our parents or preacher. However as we have gotten older, we have experimented with sin to the point of arousing curiosity, which has pulled us to deliberately go against our consciences. At this point many repent, never to sin in that area again. There are others who, rather than listening to their consciences, challenge the rule and rewrite it to suit their life-style. This is a normal process. The problem is, such persons will frequently be held prisoner to their lusts. They may never again be able to submit to an absolute standard of right and wrong: the Bible.

Outward Religious Overkill. There are many teenage wolves parading in sheep's clothing who have learned how to run around saying, "Bah, bah, praise the Lord, bah, bah," wearing Jesus belts and making the scene at all the Christian concerts. They have been known to attend Bible studies and at times even teach them. They tithe (most of the time) and usually appear bubbly and effervescent.

The problem is, they frequently slip into sexual immorality, knowing full well that it is wrong, but also claiming the Scripture, "the blood of Jesus cleanses us from all sin." They even guzzle six-packs from time to time and have a little marijuana when the reefer gets passed, but know that after all nobody is perfect.

Such brothers and sisters have little moral strength, but instead are motivated by "outward religious overkill." They feel compelled to do many outwardly Christian things to make sure that other people believe that they are saved, even though underneath they know in their own hearts they are condemned.

(If you do not think you come under this category, I want you to take another look. There are thousands all over our country who are in this bondage and are not aware of it.)

Finger Pointing and Excuses. When we feel condemned, it is almost impossible to stand alone. We often search desperately to find someone to share the blame. For some reason, standing before the firing squad alone is worse. We are all very good at blaming our moral failure on others. It does not matter whether we blame our getting drunk on our best friend who bought the booze or our having sex on the girl who wore the seductive clothing.

Countless contemporary psychologists and school counselors offer us all sorts of excuses for our own wrong behavior: the environment, our parents, or the way we were brought up. Such excuses given to us by the professionals might make us feel less guilty inside, but they also get us to think less of ourselves. If we cannot be counted on to be responsible for our own actions, but are rather like puppets on the strings of our environment, we get reduced to being dummies. All inner moral strength is gone because there is no longer any moral responsibility.

Blaming others is not the answer. When we point our fingers at someone else, we have three fingers pointing back at ourselves. Deep down we know that we share the blame.

Severe Self-condemnation. I hate to even include this fourth option, but there are those who have committed suicide out of severe self-condemnation. They were unsuccessful at killing their consciences, so they killed themselves. They considered that it would be better to be dead than to be living in the misery and torture of a condemning conscience.

There is of course another option: to repent and turn from sin. To someone who, through the teen years, has been tortured by a tyrannical conscience, that option might sound absurd. Having just reviewed all the conflict and strife that go on in young hearts, because of the conscience, it might seem impossible ever to regard the conscience as a friend. However I can honestly say my conscience is one of my best friends, and I have seen dozens of teenagers take the same steps I have taken to gain peace in their hearts and minds. Let's take a look.

9 Making Friends With Our Conscience

Guilt afflicts many young lives as the forces of good and evil battle within us. What complicates things is that we are not even sure how to tell the difference between what is right and what is wrong.

When I was entering high school, I deeply questioned the value system of our country. I wanted to know if there were absolute standards of right and wrong. I knew that my parents were "good, moral people," but why should I be good and moral? My questions were not motivated by any serious rebellion or arrogance, I simply wanted to know why:

- Why should I wait until marriage to go to bed with a girl?
- Why not cheat on exams?
- Why not steal money from the wallets of fellow students or clothes from department stores?
- Why not get drunk at parties? Everyone else does.
- Why not paint my neighbors' house red on Halloween?
- Why should I drive the speed limits?

In my search for meaning and purpose in life, as a young man I began to read the Bible. As I read I considered the possibility that there was a God and that if He did exist, He would have revealed Himself to us. In revealing Himself to us, He would have shown us the right way to live so as to protect us from harm and to allow us to function effectively. I also realized that if there was such a set of absolute standards for all people, it could not have been written by mere man, but by God, the Absolute Person. Therefore I started reading the Bible.

I am well aware that some people who read the Bible get more and more confused, but that is not what happened to me. As I read, I understood. At that point, while still a freshman in high school, I committed my life to Jesus Christ, acknowledging that He had all authority over me, and I committed myself to follow every moral standard in the Bible. I also committed myself to *not* follow any standard or moral ethic that was *not* mentioned in the Bible. I had a lot to learn, but I was willing to give myself to it. I had a very confused conscience that needed to be informed, and my teacher was going to be the Word of God.

Educating Your Conscience

The Bible has a lot to say about educating your conscience. "Do not be conformed to this world but be transformed by the renewal of your mind, that you may prove what is the will of God, what is good and acceptable and perfect" (Romans 12:2 RSV). Or, as it says in the Phillips translation, "Don't let the world around you squeeze you into its own mould, but let God re-mould your minds from within, so that you may prove in practice that the Plan of God for you is good, meets all His demands and moves towards the goal of true maturity" (YOUNG CHURCHES). Again in 1 Peter we read, "As obedient children, do not be conformed to the passions of your former ignorance" (1:14 RSV). Rather than living our lives according to the life-styles and behavior of others around us, we are to dare to live differently. Rather than following our natural instincts under the philosophy "If it feels good, do it," we are to pattern our behavior after what God says in the Bible.

If you are a Christian, you have reason to act morally; not because you are an American or because you are a goody-goody who does everything your mommy tells you, but because you are a child of God. This is the basis of morality. You are not to expect people to act ethically when they do not believe that the Bible provides a set of absolute standards. However, if you have been born again, you are a new person and must live under a new system of morals.

Soon after I became a Christian and decided to live under the biblical standards, I was asked to attend a snow camp. I always hated camps, but things were getting boring in the winter months, so I accepted the invitation. We no sooner jumped off the bus at the campgrounds than we spotted two snowmobiles sitting there. My friend looked at me, and I looked back at him. Part of a verse I had read the night before flashed through my mind: "Let the thief no longer steal...," but I easily rejected its implications. The urge overcame us, and we jumped on them and took off. We were running along the snow trail and were even making a few of our own, having a great time. We were gone for almost a half hour when, in the distance, we noticed a cloud of rumbling snow coming toward us. At first I did not think anything of it, but as it got closer, I could tell it was another snowmobile. It was being driven by an older man, and as he pulled up alongside of us, I could see the fire in his eyes. I was overwhelmed with fear. Inside I knew that I had done wrong, even though I did not have all the reasons worked out in my head. That man introduced himself to us as the director of the camp, and in a long string of stern and fiery words, he accused us of stealing and told us that we would be sent home immediately.

As we drove the snowmobiles back to camp, I recalled the verse I had been reading the night before, "Let the thief no longer steal, but rather let him labor, doing honest work with his hands ..." (Ephesians 4:28 RSV). While it was true that I never intended to steal the snowmobile, I knew that God was teaching me to listen to my educated conscience. I made up my mind that I would not make any excuses for my misconduct, but that I would submit to whatever the director said.

When we got back to camp, the director called me, my friend, and my youth minister into the recreation hall and sat us down. I was prepared to suffer the humiliation of being sent home from the camp. To my amazement, the director, after explaining to my youth pastor what had happened, suggested, "But I would be willing to allow these boys to work in the kitchen, instead of sending them home."

Wow, I said to myself, *God really is going to allow me to do "honest work with my hands"!*

"But we didn't do anything wrong," my friend burst out. "I think this whole place stinks! There's no way I'm going to clean any tables or do the dishes!" I felt bad, but my friend was asked to leave. They called his parents, and he went home. I gladly submitted to the bucket brigade, because God was teaching me to be sensitive to my newly educated conscience.

There is a popular expression, "Let your conscience be your guide." You might think that is biblical, but it is not—not exactly. Our consciences are a big help, but they are often misinformed or underinformed, in which case they could mislead us or even fail to lead us at all. A better saying would be, "Let your conscience be informed."

I have had girls come to me saying, "Wow, I didn't feel guilty when I was in the car with him, but I sure do now." Unfortunately such a testimony shows that when we are considering whether something is right or wrong, we cannot simply say, "Now let's see, does this make me feel guilty?" especially when our consciences are ignorant of God's absolute moral standards.

Therefore every Christian who sincerely wants to follow Jesus must take time every day to learn the absolute standards by reading the Bible. There is no freeze-dried morality that you can sprinkle on your cereal in the morning. "Study to shew thyself approved unto God . . ." (2 Timothy 2:15 KJV). Better than getting a B.A., B.S., M. Div., or even a Ph.D. degree, we need to study for an A.U.G. degree: Approved Unto God!

Purifying the Conscience

It is necessary for most of us to cleanse our consciences.

The apostle Paul talks about having dirty consciences, "Thus, sinning against your brethren and wounding their conscience when it is weak, you sin against Christ" (1 Corinthians 8:12 RSV). Elsewhere he talks about "deceitful liars, whose consciences are dead, as if burned with a hot iron" (*see* 1 Timothy 4:2). And again, "To the pure all things are pure, but to the corrupt and unbelieving nothing is pure; their very minds and consciences are corrupted. They profess to know God, but they deny him by their deeds; they are detestable, disobedient, unfit for any good deed" (Titus 1:15, 16 RSV). This might gross you out, but those verses describe most of us. We need to have our consciences scrubbed clean.

Sandy was an eighteen-year-old alcoholic. I met her the night after she had been raped by some dirty old man who always hung around the bars in town. She felt so dirty and unclean that she could not look me in the eye. She kept apologizing for the way she was dressed and told me that I could leave anytime I wanted to.

She told me that she hated herself and her background. "You wouldn't believe all that I have been through," she said as she rolled up her sleeve to reveal several severe scars. "I've tried to kill myself many times, but I even failed at that. What good am I? I don't have a home. I don't have a family. I don't have anybody who cares about me. What good am I? Why don't you just leave?"

The fact that I was a minister made her even more uneasy, but I could not leave. *If Jesus can't help her, then what good is the cross?* I said to myself. She saw her life as a heap of rubble that could never be put back together again, but I saw hope.

"You have tried to straighten your life out, haven't you?" She nodded in agreement as she lit her third cigarette. "Can you think of anything else to do?"

"If I could, do you think I'd be talking to you?" she puffed as she threw the matches on the table.

"Well, Sandy, I have just met you, but I believe that Jesus can help you." She smiled back at me as if to say, "This ought to be good for a laugh."

I gave her an illustration that I hoped would make sense to her. "There was a man driving one of the first cars ever made down the street. It was a Model-T Ford. The car started to sputter and spit, so he pulled over. He lifted the hood, and for hours he tried in vain to find the problem. Then another car pulled over next to him. A man hopped out and asked, 'Can I check it out?' After less than a minute he pulled his head out from under the hood of the car and told the driver, 'Hop in and start it up.' The car started immediately. Humiliated, the man got out of the car to thank the stranger, and the stranger said, 'That's okay, my name is Henry Ford, and I made that car.' " She chuckled as I proceeded to apply it to her life.

"Sandy, we all go our own way at times and get our lives messed up; it's just like driving a car through the Everglades. But God created us, and He knows how we should run the best. He has given us His Owner's Manual to tell us how we are to live."

She received what I told her. We talked for a while longer, and then I asked her, "Would you like to start life all over again and let Jesus clean you out?" God was working on her heart, and she nodded in agreement.

We prayed together, and she asked Jesus to come into her life and cleanse her. Then together we thanked God for doing it and for making her a new creature.

When I opened my eyes, I expected to see a smile, but to my surprise, there were tears running down her face. I wanted to ask why the tears, but I thought we had covered enough for one afternoon, and I did not want to confuse her.

Several weeks later, while talking to her, it was obvious that she still felt very guilty over things she had done a long time ago. She was guilty over sins that were already forgiven. So finally I asked her about those bitter tears she cried after she asked Christ to come into her life. It made me sad to hear what she said, because for the first time I saw how destructive a defiled conscience can be. Here is what she told me: "I felt too dirty for God, and I still do. God is so perfect and so clean. He doesn't want an old slut like me. I am a beat-up tramp. I'm a loser, and I will always be a loser. God might love you, but there's no way He could love me."

Her words cut through my heart. I hurt deeply because I felt inadequate to express how much God loved her, in spite of what she had done. I walked over to my stereo and played this song for her. "Listen to this," I said. She pressed her lips hopelessly together, but at least she listened.

I Don't Care Where You've Been Sleeping
Don Francisco

I loved you long before the time your eyes first saw the day
And everything I've done has been to help you on the way;
But you took all that you wanted then at last you took your leave
And traded off a Kingdom for the lies that you believed.

I don't care where you've been sleeping
I don't care who's made your bed
I already gave My life to set you free.
There's no sin you could imagine that is stronger than My love,
And it's all yours if you'll come home again to Me.

And although you've chosen darkness with its miseries and fears
Although you've gone so far from Me and wasted all those years,
Even though My name is spotted by the mire in which you lie
I'd take you back this instant if you'd turn to Me and cry.

When you come back to your senses and you see who's been to
    blame,
Remember all the good things that were yours with just My name.
Then don't waste another thought before you change the way
    you're bound
I'll be running out to meet you if you'll only turn around.

"Sandy," I said as I turned off the stereo, "Jesus loves you not
because of who *you* are, but because of who *He* is. He is love, and
He always will be love. Nothing you will ever do will cause God to
stop being love." She seemed to understand, so I continued. "If you
were a goody-goody, He wouldn't love you any more. In fact, if you
were a goody-goody, you probably wouldn't know that you needed
Him. Jesus didn't come to help straight people, but He came to help
sinners—just like me and you."

"Look at this." I showed her two verses: "For as the heavens are
high above the earth, so great is his steadfast love toward those who
fear him; as far as the east is from the west, so far does he remove

our transgressions from us" (Psalms 103:11, 12 RSV). The next day she memorized those verses and has quoted them hundreds of times since; but before the night was over, Sandy knelt on the floor, with my wife, and together they went through her past, naming and confessing all her sins. Together they claimed that her sins were under the blood of Jesus and that they were separated from her as far as the east is from the west. That night her conscience was virtually cleansed. Her face radiated with joy that came only because she was free from the tyrannical rule of her conscience. The condemning finger of all her inner guilt was no longer there. She knew what it means when the Bible says, "Happy are those whose sins are forgiven, whose wrongs are pardoned. Happy is the man whom the Lord does not accuse of doing wrong and who is free from all deceit" (Psalms 32:1, 2 TEV).

If you are a normal person, with a 98.6° temperature, there are probably things deep inside you from which you need to be set free. Your conscience needs to receive the forgiveness Jesus died to give you.

Why don't you get on your knees and talk with Jesus?

A Word for the Straight Kids

Your life might be very different from Sandy's. There are thousands of young people who have been raised in Christian homes and who have been guarded from many of the painful pitfalls of the rest of the young people in the world. If you are among this number, then you probably have two very serious problems: You are likely to hate being so straight, and you may never realize the seriousness of your own personal sinfulness.

If You Hate Being Straight. Gordon was the son of a preacher, and there was nothing he hated more than his father's occupation. He felt as if he was cursed by God to be raised in such a morally demanding home. He loved the juicy stories of his reckless friends at school, who boasted of their rebellious and immoral behavior.

One night while we were sitting in my car, talking, he actually cried because he hated the boring Christian games he was expected to play. He hated having to dress up like a pretty little boy, in a tie and jacket, twice every Sunday. He hated getting kissed by the old ladies or pinched on the cheek. He hated looking like a saint on the outside when on the inside there was nothing he wanted more than to be a sinner. In a sense, he wanted to sell his birthright in a religious family for a bowl of soup.

Have you ever felt that way? Have you envied the life-style of some of your girl friends who have looser morals and who get more dates than you do? Have you ever felt out of place on Mondays when everyone else has a sinful story to tell about the weekend? Have you ever envied the wicked and wished that you heard about Jesus after you had kicked up your heels and sown some weeds for a few years?

If so, you are in serious shape and you are not alone. There are many others who have the same problem. Listen to this:

> But I had nearly lost confidence;
>   my faith was almost gone
> because I was jealous of the proud
>   when I saw that things go well for the wicked. . . .
> They do not suffer as other people do . . . .
>   they do not have the troubles that others have.
> And so they wear pride like a necklace
>   and violence like a robe;
> Their hearts pour out evil,
>   and their minds are busy with wicked schemes.
> They laugh at other people and speak of evil things;
>   they are proud and make plans to oppress others.
> They speak evil of God in heaven
>   and give arrogant orders to men on earth,
> so that even God's people turn to them
>   and eagerly believe whatever they say.

They say "God will not know;
  the Most High will not find out."
That is what the wicked are like.
  They have plenty and are always getting more.
Is it for nothing, then, that I have kept myself pure
  and not committed sin?
O God, you have made me suffer all day long;
  every morning you have punished me.

Psalms 73:2, 4–14 TEV

To hate being so straight and to envy the wicked go hand in hand. This Hebrew poem very honestly expresses the heart of a moral man who looked jealously at the lives of the immoral. He considered his own convictions with regret, even considering forsaking holiness because God probably would never find out anyway.

Ignorance of My Sinfulness.   One night my college roommate and I were turning out the lights, getting ready to jump into our bunk beds, when he said, "Wow, you know, I have never met such a holy person as you." He obviously did not know me very well. "Do you ever sin?" he continued. "I mean, I am sure that you sin once in a while, but I'll bet you have gone all day without sinning. I'll bet you must go a whole week without sinning." I assured him that I did sin, but as I lay there in my bunk the thought ran through my mind, *I guess maybe I didn't sin today, did I?* Well, if I had not sinned up to that point, I sure did then, because I was obviously guilty of pride.

If we do not smoke, drink, chew, or go with the girls who do, we might have trouble finding sin in our lives. Many churches have a very strict list of ethics: no card playing, no makeup, no tobacco of any kind, no mixed bathing, and so on. Others have a similar list, though perhaps less strict: no drugs, no alcohol, no premarital or extramarital sex. Regardless of how strict the list is, the effect is usually the same: It subtly communicates the idea that if we are not guilty of those particular things, then we are not sinners. And when anyone is found guilty of those things, we are quick to judge and smack our lips and withdraw friendship and very slow to understand and respond to love. This is hypocrisy, and Jesus hated it. In fact such spiritual pride and smugness is what Jesus hated more than anything else. On the outside we might think that we are pure, but on the inside we are full of garbage. Worldliness is not external; it is internal.

In the 1800s a fourteen-year-old youth wrote these words as he considered "God's majesty and my sinfulness":

> I do not hesitate to say that those who examined my life would not have seen any extraordinary sin, yet as I looked upon myself I saw outrageous sin against God. I was not like other boys, untruthful, dishonest, swearing and so on. But of a sudden, I met Moses carrying the law . . . God's ten words . . . and as I read them, they all seemed to join in condemning me in the sight of the thrice holy Jehovah.

That teenager who was aware of the seriousness of his own sinfulness even though, compared to other youth, he looked like an angel, was Charles Haddon Spurgeon. He went on to become one of the greatest preachers the world has ever seen. One of the reasons God was able to use him so mightily was because even at a young age he repented of sin. Spurgeon admitted that outwardly he looked like Mr. Clean. Everyone would have thought he was nearly sinless. For years, he was obviously convinced of the same thing, but then the *Holy* Spirit of God showed him something different. From this point he gained a great love for holiness and a great hatred for sin. In many ways his potential for the Kingdom of God began when, as a teenager, he realized the seriousness of his own sinfulness. In fact, until we do see our sinfulness and hate it, Jesus will be a nice word, but we will not know His power.

Fortunately seeing our personal sinfulness is not our responsibility; it is God's. Jesus said that the Holy Spirit would come, "And when he comes, he will convince the world concerning sin and righteousness and judgment" (John 16:8 RSV).

If your eyes are still blind to the fact that your sins nailed Jesus to the cross, then I want you to say this to God:

Jesus,

I am self-righteous. In fact I am so self-righteous that I can't even see what a creep I am. I know that the Bible says that I am a sinner, and I know that somewhere in my heart there are piles of sin that would make a garbage dump look like an ant hill, but I can't see it. You say that You came for sinners, not for saints, so please knock the self-righteous wind out of me and take the blinders off my eyes. I at least began by admitting that I am proud, so please forgive me for that. I do humble myself, and I believe that You will help me see what a worm I really am in comparison to You. Thanks for loving me even when I am so confused. Amen.

Even David prayed a similar prayer:

> No one can see his own errors;
> Deliver me, Lord, from *hidden faults!*
> Keep me safe, also, from willful sins;
> don't let them rule over me.
>
> Psalms 19:12, 13 TEV, *italics added*

And elsewhere he asked:

> Examine me, O God, and know my mind;
> test me, and discover my thoughts.
> Find out if there is any evil in me
> and guide me in the everlasting way.
>
> Psalms 139:23, 24 TEV

Your life does not have to be full of problems or your arms full of holes from heroin needles before you recognize your sinfulness. It is as much a miracle for God to deliver you from pride as it is to be delivered from prostitution. It takes as much help from God to overcome gossiping as it does to overcome swearing; in fact it often takes more.

Rather than hating holiness, God wants us to love it. For those who have been raised in strict, ethical homes, God says, "Congratulations!" He tells us, "I want to see you experts in good, and not even beginners in evil" (Romans 16:19 PHILLIPS).

Be sure to treat your conscience as your best friend.

1. When you do things that are wrong, how do you react to your conscience?
2. What are some ways that we make excuses for our immoral behavior?
3. Why are we sometimes afraid to be called "holy"?
4. Why is it important, as teenagers, to be able to say with Charles Spurgeon, "I know I am a sinner"?
5. Why is it important to make friends with our consciences?

1. Has anyone felt like Sam, who was sick of going through the cycles of pleasing his Christian friends and then pleasing his non-Christian friends?

2. Do you know anyone who has apparently killed his or her conscience? How would you describe this person?
3. What does it mean to educate your conscience?
4. Are the following words good or bad? *holy, pure, puritanical.*
   How would you like to be known by these words?

10 "Life Is a Drag"

You may yawn, but a silent disease that crawls through classrooms, corridors, and cafeterias is boredom. It is a fatal disease that has caused many to do crazy and self-destructive things.

I live in a town south of Miami, Florida, called Homestead. Homestead has all the heat of the south, but unlike many towns in Florida, there is no beach. Some swim in the slimy canals or the condemned rock pit where every year several lose their lives. Apart from the bowling alley and the roller rink, there is not much recreation, so the kids call it Deadstead. With a lot of spare time and little to do, our area has become known as the "drugstore to the nation." Pot, Quaaludes, and coke have become much of the entertainment.

Adolescence is a time when we have more energy than we will ever again have in our lives, and that energy must be channeled somewhere. If it is not used constructively, it will be used to destroy. When a kid is not given something good to do, you cannot just pull the plug and expect him to sit there. You can be sure a teenager will find *something* to do.

Television

According to *Newsweek,* before a young person graduates from high school, he will have watched an average of 15,000 hours of television, 18,000 murders (more than 1 for every hour of TV watched), and 350,000 commercials. This means that every week a youth has spent an average of 42 hours sitting in front of the pacifying blue screen—or 50 percent more time in front of a TV than in the classroom. The only activity that takes more teenage time than TV is sleeping. No wonder there is such boredom.

When I was in graduate school, I had a classmate who watched

TV eleven hours a day. He could tell you everything that was happening on all the programs and would frequently watch more than one TV at a time. I often wondered why he bothered interrupting his viewing to go to class.

The problems caused by television are enormous. Let's look at a few of them.

Mental Mush. The TV is not called the "boob tube" for nothing. It is turning young minds to mush.

The average person is said to have an 80 percent boredom factor. This means that he is using only 20 percent of his brain. To pore passively over the visual images of TV hardly develops any brain power. If we spend an average of eight hours a day sleeping and five hours watching TV, we are wasting more than half of every day in nonactivity.

I heard of a teenager who was given a book for Christmas last year. He spent all day looking for the place to put the batteries.

Adolescence is meant to be a time of creative development. A research team from the University of Southern California has noted a marked drop-off in creative skills among young people and has blamed it on TV. Malcolm Muggeridge, a well-known English atheist who has been converted to Christianity, was quoted as saying, "Television has so affected the minds of the American public that a totalitarian government could easily move in."

TV viewing also has distorted reality. Young and old alike are conditioned to think that what they see on TV is the way things really are. Pathetically TV has become the parent, the prophet, and the priest in the average American home. "If it is okay for TV, it is okay for me" is a subtle statement that we have all consciously or unconsciously made. *Newsweek* magazine has said, "Television has become perhaps the most potent influence on the beliefs, attitudes, values and behavior of those who are being raised in its all-pervasive glow."

Young people are not the only ones who are getting a distorted perception of reality. It was reported that last year "Marcus Welby,

M.D." received 2.5 million letters requesting medical advice. Children are not sending those letters to a fictional doctor; these are adults whose brains are being turned into boobs by the boob tube.

Moral Mush. Moral and human values are denied, program after program, on all the major networks. The value of a human life is denied more than a thousand times every year, every time a person is fictitiously killed. For every divorce, affair, or immoral escapade, the value of one's virginity is seriously doubted. Sex and violence have distorted the personal convictions of many young people and have eroded their standards.

Several years ago, when the moral quality of the programs began to slip seriously, the networks developed what was called the Family Hour, which lasts until 9:00 P.M. Presumably, all the younger folk should be in bed at that time, when more sensual and erotic programs can be shown. The Neilson ratings have shown that there are 10.5 million young people under the age of twelve still watching after the suggested nine o'clock curfew. This indicates that 10.5 million young people are being exposed to garbage that neither they nor their parents should be watching.

Much of the programming is so violent that many young minds are being corrupted. Even eight out of ten children's programs are said to contain violence. Prison inmates have given this reason for being video buffs: "We've got the best minds in Hollywood writing our material for when we get out."

There are some who still ignorantly argue that watching violence does not reproduce violence in us. This is proven wrong almost every week. Following Evil Knievel's Snake Canyon jump, hospitals and doctors' offices all over the country were filled with broken teenage bones. In February 1976, the night after CBS aired a movie dramatically showing a gang taking over a subway train, five kids ages sixteen to nineteen entered the subway in Brooklyn, terrorized passengers, and victimized an eight-months-pregnant woman.

Television teaches cheap sex and cheap life and practically no moral values. It has become very much a false prophet, an unfaithful parent, and a demonic priest.

Physical Mush. Recently a mother told her son that his friend was at the door, asking if he would like to go skiing. "Tell him I'm busy," he replied. "I'm watching a skiing competition on TV."

Watching television has been called "the most popular indoor sport in America." I disagree. It is not a sport at all. To anyone who insists that it is a sport, I say that it is constantly guilty of unsportsmanlike conduct: It plays dirty, making up its own rules, and never gives its opponents a chance to compete. Even its own teammates are left sitting on the bench.

There is a real problem when we prefer sitting on the bench, watching life being acted out for us, to actually getting involved in activity. When we get to the point where we prefer watching baseball on TV to going outside to play ball, or prefer watching a party on TV to going to a party, or even prefer watching church on TV to going to church, we have become addicted to an opiate that is killing us with boredom. It guarantees to turn our muscles to mush and our fitness to flab.

Social Mush. A mother, when she asked her son if he would like to have some friends over to watch TV, was told, "No, mom, if I had friends over, I would have to talk to them, and that would mean I might miss part of my programs."

This might seem overdramatized, but it is a true story. If you have never said anything like that or if you would never dream of such a thing, take a more self-critical look. Frequently when you sit down in front of the TV, you are choosing against writing a letter, calling a friend, or going to someone's house. In fact, frequently, TV becomes an escape from social interaction. No one on the TV will ever jump off the screen and tell you they do not like the way your breath smells or the way you comb your hair, but a friend might. No one on the TV will ever make you feel insecure. After all, most of the characters on TV are perfectly predictable. However, being involved with your friends is more risky. At times they will make you feel threatened and insecure. They will tell you things about yourself they do not like, and they will be challenging. But don't worry, TV will hide you from all that.

Yes, TV is a great escape from life. It is so easy to hide your insecurities behind the glass screen, knowing you are safe. You are safe from getting mocked by a cynical friend. Safe from losing friends because even though a program might go off the air, a new one will be there to take its place. Safe from all the potential dangers of real, live people. Safe and bored!

Other Bloodsuckers

Hey, television is not the only monster that eats up the strength and vitality of young people. Books can do the same thing.

Obviously nothing is wrong with reading books, but I have talked with many young people who have told me that they hide behind page after page of novels, especially love stories or science fiction. Both types of books have one thing in common: They let the readers escape from their worlds. To move into someone else's romance is to temporarily leave your own heartaches behind. To leave planet Earth for the world of outer space gives many the opportunity to forget about their broken homes or crumbling worlds.

Drugs, another so-called solution, feed boredom, instead of fighting it. Like TV, they provide us with sensations without our having to become personally involved. Such passive solutions to boredom only create greater problems and an even greater boredom factor. Rather than actually dealing with boredom, we only feel less bored, in which case our feelings are lying to us.

Moviemakers know that kids look to the theater to relieve much of their boredom and therefore gear much of their production toward youth. Although people between the ages of twelve and twenty-four make up only 29 percent of the population, they account for 59 percent of all the moviegoing public. Going to the theater to see a movie does involve an activity that at least gets you out of the house, but unfortunately it is an activity that plops you in a seat for at least two hours, with nothing to do but act like a sponge and soak it in or get up and go to the rest room. It does not provide a lasting cure for teenage boredom.

I know dozens of kids who hide from boredom in nature, taking daily trips into the forest, going fishing, or even collecting butterflies. Obviously nature activities can be highly stimulating. However when we are involved in such hobbies every single day, to the exclusion of any other activities, there is reason for concern. Also when we go off, day after day, all by ourselves, there are probably deep pockets of boredom that are more severe and painful than anyone might realize; and most likely we are not talking to anyone about it.

The list goes on and on, but whether it be the TV set, books, drugs, alcohol, or even Mother Nature, you cannot deal with boredom by running away and hiding from it. Boredom needs to be eliminated. Teenage years must not be wasted warming the bench in front of your TV or sucking marijuana smoke into your young lungs. Your brain is at its peak, and your lungs are too pure. Youth is a time to grab for all the life you can. As our friend Solomon has said:

> Be happy, young man, while you are young,
> and let your heart give you joy in the days of your youth. . . .
> Ecclesiastes 11:9 NIV

The problem is that many young people do not know where to look for happiness.

Boredom is when you are aware of all the things you are not doing. Boredom is when you feel like Pepsi without the fizz or pretzels without the salt. Boredom is sitting on the bench when you practiced as hard as everyone else the rest of the week. Boredom is not having enough motivation to even cheat on an exam, let alone study for it. It is when you are too lazy to make friends or else too lazy to talk when you are with them. Boredom fastens itself to teenagers like a leech and sucks blood, leaving many tired and unmotivated. Youth is meant to be a time of enthusiasm and creative activity. It is a time to develop mentally, morally, physically, and socially, but boredom kills all that. When we feel bored, we need more than a slice of Wonder Bread or a slug of Geritol.

11 "What Am I Doing Here?"

One of the question marks that keeps popping up in teenage minds is, "What am I doing here?"

As a child, people frequently asked me the question, "What are you going to do when you grow up?" When I was four I would quickly answer, "I'm going to be a fireman." When I was five, I would respond, "I'm going to be a baseball player." At six I said, "I'm going to be president of the United States"—pretty ambitious! When I was seven, I said, "I want to drive a truck." Between eight and nine, I wanted to be a fisherman. When I was ten and eleven, I went back to baseball. When I was twelve, I began to think a lot harder about the question, but would usually answer it by saying, "I hope to play pro football."

Then when I was thirteen, I sat down with my high-school guidance counselor. He looked over his bifocals and asked the question I had heard so many times in the past, though this time it caused me to feel very uneasy: "What are you going to do with your life?" My mind raced from the fireman to the baseball player to the president of the United States, and nothing seemed believable. His question made me doubt who I was, and that rattled me. He chuckled graciously and told me that most teenagers did not know what they were going to do with their lives, but somehow that did not help my feelings of insecurity. I confessed, "I really don't know what I'm going to do."

My guidance counselor's question that afternoon drove me to ask an even larger question, "What am I doing here?" I wanted more than a good-paying job, because underneath I knew that there must be more to life than big bucks. I wanted more than public recognition, because I knew that fame and popularity would eventually disappear, like the morning dew. I needed a reason to live and purpose for being alive. After finding meaning to my own life, I knew that I would gain the direction that I desired.

The Four Biggest Decisions in Life

Before most people leave their teenage years, they are faced with making the four biggest decisions they will make in their entire lives. Business and professional people pride themselves on the vital decisions they so effortlessly make every day. The decisions that they face are nothing compared to those teenagers face.

The decisions teenagers make determine the course their lives will take. They are not dealing with big bucks or making payrolls; they are working with their futures. These four major decisions are:

1. What *vocation* will I enter?
2. Where will I go to *college?*
3. Who will I *marry?*
4. What will I do with *Jesus Christ?*

No decisions will ever be more important to you than these, and most people make them before they say good-bye to their teen years.

It hurts to be a teenager entering into adult life with no answers to the questions of ultimate meaning and purpose in life. Acquiring money, raising a respectable family, even providing for children will not fulfill the deepest needs in the human heart.

Jesus, when He considered the ultimate values in life, asked, "So what good is it if you gain the whole world and forfeit your own soul?" (*see* Matthew 16:26). In one respect, until we are able to die, we are not ready to live. Until our existence here on earth makes sense in light of all eternity, we need to keep asking the question, "What am I doing here?"

Hunger Pains

While asking questions about the meaning and purpose of life, young people frequently find an emptiness in their bellies, for which they have no answer.

A nineteen-year-old girl returned to her home in Connecticut after the first semester at college. She locked herself in her room and cried. Her parents tried to reason with her but they got no response. "Honey, what is wrong?" they futilely asked. "We have given you everything in life. You have your own car; you have a fine stereo; you have always had plenty of girl friends and boyfriends. We have sent you to the finest schools; we have always given you plenty of spending money and taken you with us on vacations. We have certainly not abused you in any way. Honey, please, tell us, what is wrong?" Finally, after three days she responded through her tears, "I want something, but I don't know what it is."

Have you ever felt that way? As if you wanted something, but you did not know what it was? Blaise Pascal, French physicist and philosopher of the seventeenth century, said in *Pensées,* "The heart has its reasons which reason knows nothing of." Again he said, "There is a God-shaped vacuum in the heart of every man which cannot be filled by any created thing, but only by God the Creator, made known through Jesus Christ."

There is no peace like the peace that comes when you have peace with God. This marks the beginning of a brand-new life, and it is essential to have such an intimate relationship with the eternal God before you begin making other monumental decisions. Before you answer the temporal question, "What am I going to do with my life?" you must answer the eternal question, "What am I doing here?" Jesus gives you a foundation upon which to build the rest of your life. You still might not know what you are going to do with your life, but at least that is not so threatening anymore. As someone has wisely said, "Although I don't know what the future holds, I know the One who holds the future."

Jesus said, "Seek ye first the kingdom of God, and His righteousness; and all these things shall be added unto you" (Matthew 6:33, KJV). Until you are prepared to die, you are not ready to live. But with Jesus we will never die.

If you are a teenager, this is the time to give yourself to Jesus and to recognize that He has given Himself to you. Solomon has said, "Remember also your Creator in the days of your youth, before the evil days come, and the years draw nigh, when you will say, 'I have no pleasure in them' " (Ecclesiastes 12:1 RSV). Do not waste years trying to live life apart from the Source of life: Jesus! Before you are old and burned out and you have nothing to offer God, other than your knitting needles and rocking chair, make your decision for Christ.

> Just one life 'twill soon be past,
> Only what's done for Christ will last.

If you have a hunger deep in your soul and if you have wanted to know for certain that you are a child of God, I encourage you to pray this prayer:

> Dear Jesus, I sure have waited a long time to do this. I guess I have been afraid, but I don't want to wait any longer. Right now I thank You that You died on the cross to take away the sin that stood between us. Thanks for rising from the dead and for being right here with me now. Please come into my life and clean me out. Live inside me; set up Your home inside me. I will do whatever You want me to do. Praise You, Lord.

If you have talked with Jesus and have received Him into your life, then let me be the first to welcome you into God's family. You are a new person. You will notice that you will have new desires and new motivation, because Jesus will be taking over certain areas and making some radical changes. Most important you now know that when you die, you will go to be with Jesus. Actually you will never die. Jesus has turned death into a birth canal through which we move from one phase of life into another. And until we pass into the next phase of life, we have a reason to be here; we have a purpose to life. Life ceases to be a soap opera between lousy commercials; it becomes challenging and stimulating. Jesus gets us headed down the path of life, and there are always exciting things to do. Most significantly He is with us every inch of the way. He helps make the other big decisions in life. Everything is easier once we take care of the biggest decision: "What will I do with Jesus?" Once we receive Him, He answers the "then what?" He also answers the "so what?" Jesus is the so-what of life.

12 The Rest of My Life

Ask yourself this question: "When my name gets chiseled on a tombstone, what do I want to be remembered by?"

When Chris Evert started high school, she deeply wanted to be a cheerleader, but she had to make a choice between cheerleading and tennis. If she had known then that she would win the U.S. Open five times and Wimbledon twice, the choice might have been easier. However we must realize at the time she was just an average (perhaps above-average) kid who wanted to be a normal teenager with the acceptance of her friends at school. Cheerleading was a good way to gain it. She explains that the choice was not easy, "But I made my choice. When I was just about Clare's age [her younger sister], maybe a year older, about fourteen, I wanted in the worst way to be a cheerleader. All my friends were trying out. I went to two tryouts and thought I was pretty good."

Chris says that her dad gave her good advice in the matter, " 'You can either be a great player or you can be a cheerleader and go to all the parties and turn out to be an average player' . . . I'm sorry I wasn't a cheerleader. But I couldn't have done that and won five U.S. Opens and two Wimbledons." Referring to her dad, she says, "The thing I like the most is that he never told me what to do. He let me choose."

That choice that Chris Evert made while yet a teenager was probably the single greatest choice ever made for the advancement of women's sports. When she was fourteen, she had the guts to "go for it"! She laid aside most of the thrills and frills of common teenage life. In fact she only attended one prom and one slumber party throughout her high-school days. But she had a higher goal and has reached a higher glory than most of her ho-hum classmates. She chose to temporarily forgo some of the kicks, to eventually achieve more lasting and permanent satisfaction.

When asked about goals, she says:

> Mastery . . . to be as good as I possibly can be. I mean, it's
> not absolutely necessary to win. I know that when I do my
> best, ninety-nine percent of the time I'll win. *I wish I could
> tell young people that.* It is hard to put it, but if I could be re-
> membered, I'd like to be . . . well, an example that any goal
> is reachable even without enormous talent. I don't have the
> athleticism of Evonne Goolagong or the strength of Martina
> Navratilova or all the things that made Billie Jean King so
> great. But I can concentrate better than anybody. I can think
> positively.

Well, Chris, you are an example to young people everywhere.
You had a goal. You went for it, and you got it. Cheerleading,
proms, and slumber parties were laid aside, but your achievements
have more than paid you back for all that.

Goals Worth Striving For

Every healthy teenager needs something for which he can give his
life. Every teenager longs for a cause to fight for, something to believe in. Not having any definite direction or any motivation allows
boredom to become a teenage termite, eating away at the most
formative, vital years of life. If the teenage years can be eaten away,
then we will be left without much hope for adult life.

The opposite of boredom is *enthusiasm.* The word *enthusiasm* is a
combination of the two Greek words, *en-theos,* which means "in
God." The cure for boredom is to be found "in God," through His
Son, Jesus.

Jesus is the source of vitality. He says, ". . . I came that they may
have life, and have it abundantly" (John 10:10 RSV). Elsewhere He
says, "I am the way, and the truth, and the life . . ." (John 14:6 RSV).
The Bible makes it perfectly explicit when it says, "He who has the

Son has life; he who has not the Son of God has not life" (1 John 5:12). Perhaps everyone you know who claims to be a follower of Jesus looks like a lemon sucker, but I have news for you: Lemon suckers make Jesus as sad as they make you. Anyone who ever told you that Jesus came to take the fun out of life is a liar. On the contrary Jesus came to give life. He alone can give the gusto to life for which every teenager is hungry.

As a young person, the choice is yours; either you can spend your life for that which is temporal—making a lot of money, building a name for yourself in the eyes of others, or even raising a handsome family—or you can live your life for that which is eternal. Now is the time to decide.

"But I Am Too Young?" *Garbage!*

It is a common misconception that teenagers are useless to God. We have heard a lot of preaching about how much Jesus loved children, and the words "Suffer little children, and forbid them not, to come unto me" (Matthew 19:14 KJV) have been all but worn out. We know that God uses grown men and women. But teenagers often fall through the slots and feel left out of the action. A fatal error that many parents and youth workers make is to treat teenagers like babies. They are not babies; they are rapidly maturing and often have more energy to use for the Kingdom of God than most adults.

Jeremiah thought that being a teenager disqualified him from God's service. God explicitly told Jeremiah, "I chose you before I gave you life, and before you were born I selected you to be a prophet to the nations," but the young man objected because of his age. He said, "... Lord, I don't know how to speak; I am too young" (Jeremiah 1:5, 6 TEV).

If you have ever felt too young for God to use, you need to hear God's words to Jeremiah as though they were spoken personally to you.

> Do not say that you are too young, but go to the people I
> send you to, and tell them everything I command you to say.
> Do not be afraid of them, for I will be with you to protect
> you. I, the Lord, have spoken!
>
> Jeremiah 1:7, 8 TEV

A young man was listening to a challenging speaker say, "The world has yet to see what one man full yielded to God can do." That young man jumped up and said, "By God's grace I will be that man." The man who responded was D. L. Moody.

Moody began preaching and was used by God to lead thousands, around the world, to Christ. Once, while preaching in England, he interrupted himself in mid thought. He felt the Holy Spirit was impressing something on his heart. He pointed to a teenager in the crowd, told him that God was calling him to be an evangelist, and then continued preaching. Soon after that, God raised up that youth to be a British evangelist: Rodney "Gipsy" Smith.

From young men and women God has raised up great servants. Do not put off making your decision to follow Christ. Purpose now to lay up for yourself treasures in heaven and do not fiddle your youth away, playing little games.

Jesus was a teenager once, too. When He was fourteen, he had many choices to make regarding sports, proms, parties, and so on. Near the end of his high-school days, when he was seventeen, he was aware of what He wanted His life to stand for. There would be much that He would have to sacrifice, but He decided to go for it.

Here is a song that a close friend of mine wrote:

Preparation
Ray Fowler

He was only seventeen living in a world of gray.
He had faced so many trials and temptations on the way,
But His life was halfway over. There was no time to delay.
He must be ready for the future, ready for the Day.

Many times He must have felt He could not carry on.
No one understood Him, no one else could sing His song.

But He had a Source of strength that helped Him not to stray.
And He relied upon it always, thus preparing for the Day.

He walked the lonely path of love; yes, He walked it all alone.
Popularity was not His goal; the world was not His home.
He walked that He might free us, for this He had to pay.
He was betrayed, denied, forsaken, when He died for us that Day.

But death was not victorious; His life it could not slay.
It could not kill His love so glorious.
His life was spent in preparation and He was ready for the Day.

I get tired of fooling 'round, and playing Christian games.
Jesus bought me with His blood. He's already staked the claim.
Jesus loves us, and He wants to take us home with him to stay.
But He can't if we're not ready, when He comes for us that Day.

As a teenager, Jesus faced decisions that would influence the rest of His life. He had obviously never seen a tennis racket, nor did Wimbledon ever cross His mind. But He was preparing for the day when He would face the enemy of our souls and sacrifice Himself on the Tree for our sins. He determined, as a young man, to do something that no one else in the entire world could do. He went for it, and He did it.

If you are a Christian teenager, I want you to know that the same Jesus who prepared Himself during His teenage years is living inside you. And because He is living inside you, He can help you prepare yourself. Now is the time for you to decide whether you will spend your life laying up treasure on earth or treasure in heaven.

A high-school friend of mine who decided to live for Jesus said that he would do anything God wanted him to do. The Lord told him to preach every day in the men's room. (How would you like that for your pulpit?) After he came up with 1,001 excuses for not obeying God, one day he took his Bible to school; walked into the crowded men's room, where his old friends were smoking grass and tobacco; and started to tell them about Jesus. He used to be right there with them, blowing the weed, so they listened attentively. Before long, rather than saying, "You want to go smoke?" the guys would ask each other, "Hey, you want to go hear the preacher?" He built up quite a daily congregation, and many kids who would never have known about Jesus were able to respond to Him. After a month or so the school newspaper carried an article entitled "Bathroom Crusade" (*Panther Prints* II, no. 4 [November 16, 1975]).

> In an interview . . . this reporter asked why he preaches in the boy's room . . . "When I was young, I got into drugs pretty heavily. About three years ago I met Jesus Christ and discovered that I could rely better on God than on drugs. Drugs provide only a few hours of enjoyment or fulfillment while reliance on God is more self-fulfilling."

The article concludes by saying:

> His influence has grown and there are now one or more "bathroom preachers" who preach and hand out pamphlets . . . between periods. Have a problem? Slip into a boys' room next period (unless you're a girl) and maybe you will catch one of our "bathroom preachers."

Obviously God does not call everyone to preach in the boys' room (or the girls' room, for that matter). In fact He does not even call everyone to preach. But He does expect us to make it our goal to tell others about Jesus. The time has come when we can no longer go to school as students. We must go to school as missionaries!

Glen will put us all to shame. When he started seventh grade, he was one of two Christians in his class. He purposed with the other Christian to share his faith with everyone in his homeroom. After a few months, several of his classmates had become Christians. Before long, he was teased by many, being called names like Preacher Man and Holy Glen, but the names did not slow him down. After a while those who mocked the loudest also got saved. By the time the spring came, all but two in his class had become Christians. You can be sure that there was hardly a dull moment for Glen. He was one of the most energetic young men I have seen.

The apostle Paul had a close teenage friend whose name was Timothy. This young man, like many of us, struggled with people looking down on him because he was so young. Paul told Timothy not to let it bother him.

> Don't let anyone look down on you because you are young, but set an example for the believers in speech, in life, in love, in faith and in purity.
>
> 1 Timothy 4:12 NIV

Adolescence is not simply a time we are supposed to survive, but it is a time when God wants us to thrive. He wants to harness all our energies and channel them for creative and constructive purposes. He wants these teenage days to be full of growth and development. He does not want them wasted.

Most teenagers do not need to be kicked in the pants too hard to get them to do something. Usually there are huge amounts of energy on reserve whenever something exciting is suggested. Teenagers are often like twelve-foot boats with one-hundred-horsepower outboards. The only problem is that they frequently lack direction, not knowing where or how to channel their energy.

It is time for you to make your decision. Joshua said at the end of his life, "... choose this day whom you will serve ..." (Joshua 24:15 RSV). Jesus said, "No one can serve two masters; for either he will hate the one and love the other, or he will be devoted to the one and despise the other. You cannot serve God and mammon" (Matthew 6:24 RSV). The decision is yours.

An Example From History

Young people are important to the work of God in our country and around the world. One of the mightiest revivals the United States has ever seen started among a group of teenagers in the small town of Northampton, Massachusetts.

The kids in the town frequently hung out at the local pub, staying out till all hours of the night and engaging in many immoral activities. They had no respect for their parents and would quickly rebel against all authority. They would never attend church and would busy themselves with loose and lustful pleasures. The teenagers would frequently get involved in vandalism, with little regard for the law.

Then God dramatically seized their attention:

> A young man in the bloom of his youth; who being violently seized with a pleurisy, and taken immediately very delirious, died in about two days; which . . . much affected the young people.

Jonathan Edwards described the beginning of the revival this way:

> In the fall of the year I proposed it to the young people, that they should agree among themselves to spend the evenings after lectures in social religion, and to that end divide themselves into several companies to meet in various parts of the town; which was accordingly done, and those meeting have since continued, and the example imitated by elder people.

After the Holy Spirit worked in the hearts of young people, the effect was contagious and Christians everywhere took heed to what God was doing among the young.

> Presently upon this, a great and earnest concern about the great things of religion, and the eternal world, became universal in all parts of the town, and among the persons of all degrees and all ages.

Not only did the older Christians in that immediate area stand up and take notice, but throughout all of New England the revival fires spread as the news of young lives getting turned on to Jesus was told from town to town. The revival from this one small group of young people in the town of Northampton contributed to what is known in history as the Great Awakening.

Boredom in a Group

I have been in some youth groups that are so encrusted with boredom that any enthusiasm is treated with great hatred and spite. Like the youth group in Northampton, Massachusetts, they got more excited about sneaking a smoke behind the church than sitting through some preacher's worn-out "snooze material." Some kids take the attitude, "Go ahead, just try to have fun. We'll show you that it will flop. No matter what you do, you are wasting your time."

There is one sure way to crack through such a crust: Act as if God were God. If God is God, then all our God talk is more than just hot air. Any youth group can be turned upside down and all boredom be cast like a mountain into the sea if we consider the fact that God is God, and that, as God, He has something challenging for us.

For months I worked myself weary over a youth group in Illinois. No matter what we did, I could not get more than a few kids out for any activities. I offered them a free trip to a museum in Chicago, and only two kids showed up. All they wanted was a free lunch. Another night we went to a concert; four went just to get out of the house. It seemed that no matter what I attempted, they never showed an enthusiastic response. It was as if they wanted to teach me that it was impossible to break through their boredom.

Finally I asked God for some help. He gave me an idea. On Sunday I announced that the next Friday night we would all meet at the church to go to the local teen hangout to talk to kids about Jesus. I asked everyone to bring their Bibles. You should have seen their faces! There was never such silence in a youth meeting. Their faces looked as if I had invited them for a communion service in Jonestown. I guess they thought it might mean the end of their lives—at least their social lives. They did not say much the rest of the evening. They left the church in silence, single file, looking at one another with near expressionless faces, as if to ask, "Is he for real?"

I pulled up to the church that Friday night, with my Bible and a handful of tracts, thinking I might be the only one there. It would not have been the first time I had been stood up by the group. When I pulled up, I could hardly believe my eyes. The parking lot was full of kids—twenty-five to thirty! They were doing doughnuts in the parking lot, standing on cars, and swinging from trees to release some of the energy that was charged up within them. I did not care; at least a little mild recklessness was better than apathy. For some of them, for the first time in their lives they were challenged with the fact that Jesus was something more than a word by which to fall asleep. For the first time Jesus was an issue. He was a cause who demanded not only a Friday night, but who might even demand them to lay down their reputations. To go to the local teen hangout, like a bunch of missionaries, was more than challenging; it was driving them out of their skins.

I can remember overhearing several of them saying, "There's no way I'm going to take my Bible in there." "Let's watch Fred make a fool out of himself." I really did not care what they said; the significant thing was that they were there and that they were psyched!

That night as we walked up to the front door you have never seen such a howling pack of wolves turn into such a flock of lambs. They were fighting to hide behind one another, pulling their collars up high and their hats down low. Incognito was the only way to go. But, regardless, they went!

I was in a group of teenagers north of Boston who took seriously the fact that God was actually God. One night when we were on our knees, the kids got an increasing desire to distribute a Bible to every student in the high school. In order to hand one to each of their classmates, somehow we had to come up with 1,000 Bibles. It seemed like an impossibility. However since God by definition specializes in the impossible, we prayed about it. Each of the fifteen kids got three others to pray with us, so we had almost fifty people praying for the 1,000 Bibles.

A month later I was walking along, and a man came up to me and said, "Someone told me that you are looking for some Bibles. I have four hundred. Would that be of any help to you?"

Praise God! We got in his car and immediately went to pick them up. They were the most beautiful Bibles I had ever seen. We had our share of hooting and stomping when those Bibles sat in the middle of the room where we first met for prayer.

A few months later I received a letter from a man in New York City, who worked for the American Bible Society, saying that he had 600 Bibles he would like to give us. Glory to God! The young people, who believed that God was God and was able to do anything, grew in faith and enthusiasm for the things of God, because they stepped out on Him and found that He was really there.

How about you? What difference does your life make? Ask yourself this question: "If I died this week, how would I be remembered?"

Veterans Day was over now,
All had left, and I was alone.
I began to read the names and dates
Chiseled there on every stone,
The dates which showed whether it was Mom or Dad,
Or daughter or baby son.
The dates were different, but the amount the same,
There were two on every one.
It was then I noticed something,
It was but a simple line.
It was the dash between the dates placed there,
It stood for—time.
All at once it dawned on me,
How important that little line.
The dates placed there belong to God,
But that line is yours and mine.

It's God Who gives this precious life,
And God Who takes away.
But that line—He gives to us
To do with what we may.
We know God's written the first date down
Of each and every one,
And we know those hands will write again,
For the last date has to come.
We know He'll write the last date down,
And soon—for some.
But upon the line between my dates,
I hope He'll write—"Well done."

You might be a bored kid in a dead youth group, but I have news for you: Jesus is alive, and He has something challenging for you to do. You can wait until you are old and bald before you use your energies to serve Jesus, but then you will only be able to knit afghans for the missionaries. Why not give Him all you've got now? Go for it!

1. What do you do when you're bored?
2. Do you know, without any doubt, that you will go to heaven when you die? On what basis?
3. When Jesus was a teenager, what was He probably doing to get ready for the future?

4. Write three things about yourself you would like people to remember you by, after you are gone.

1. How much TV do you watch each week? What sort of shows? Why?
2. What negative effects can TV have?
3. List five healthy guidelines to put on your TV watching.
4. Rate your youth group from one to ten (one = cold, five = luke-warm, ten = hot). What are you doing of eternal value?
5. Prayerfully chose a project that will permanently remove all boredom in your group.

13 Fake Painkillers

It is impossible to make it through the teenage years without having to deal with deep pain. No one can say he has never hurt, that everything in life is perfect. But why do some young people manage to overcome their pain and trouble, while others are destroyed by them?

In the more than ten years I have worked with teens, I have noticed a pattern in those who have become heavily involved in drugs, sex, alcohol, and the other fake painkillers the world offers: Most of them have had to deal with hard-core pain.

What do you do when you hurt so badly you could scream? Where do you turn when the pain is at its worst? You can't just ignore it; it doesn't go away! While those who have suffered common pain may be able to wait for tomorrow, hoping that things will improve, when you face hard-core pain, you know you need a solution. The hurting teenager has to reach for something. Pain is rejected by the human psyche. When exposed to it, we will reach for anything that will give us relief.

Let us briefly consider a few fake painkillers that are popular.

Alcohol

Bottles on billboards all over this country cry out to innocent teenagers, "Hey, I'll relieve your pain." An Associated Press report calculates, "an estimated 3.3 million youths aged fourteen to seventeen have problems associated with alcohol." "ABC Evening News" said that at the University of Florida, nine out of ten students drink once a week, and one out of five miss class because they drink too much. At the University of Miami, sociology professor Roger Dunham revealed in a survey that 25 percent of the students were heavy drinkers. There are a lot of hurting students reaching for some sort of relief.

Drugs

Joints, ludes, and junk have not appeared on any billboards yet, but they do not have to; they are already the largest industry in the state of Florida. A conservative estimate suggests that in south Florida the drug traffic amounts to an annual gross of about $7 billion. I live near Miami, Florida, which is known as the "drugstore to the nation." The drug traffic is only getting worse. In 1979, 857 pounds of cocaine were seized in the Miami area, but in 1980 that figure skyrocketed to 3,907 pounds.

Last summer, on the way to a convention, I sat next to two big-time junkies on the airplane. They were on their way back from a large rock festival in Kingston, Jamaica. Although I sought for an opportunity to gain circumstantial evidence to report them, I found none. They were too smooth. They had made it twice around customs without being checked, and they were high on the fact that "the pigs" were so easy to sneak past. One of them was reading an article on the ills of marijuana. It enraged them to hear what the opposition had to say. They laughed at the solutions that were suggested, insisting that to resist marijuana was to fight a losing battle. I do not get airsick, but that day I felt nauseated, sitting next to two men who thought they were peddling *painkillers* to kids, when in reality they were selling *kid killers.*

The most talked-about surge in drug use took place during the war in Vietnam, and it continues in the military. In 1978 a congressional task force toured troops in West Germany and came back with data they were afraid to make public: An estimated 80 to 90 percent were "using hashish *frequently.*"

Why so much dope in the military? The answer is obvious: They use so much dope because they feel so much pain. Vietnam was a painful experience for the GIs, and they needed something. When you hurt badly, you either have to get rid of the pain or deaden the senses so that you do not feel as much.

Sex

Sex, for a teenager, has always been confusing, but now it is worse than ever. Like a little beer or some marijuana, sex appeals to many because it is at least a momentary release from an otherwise impersonal, cold world. Even though young people know there should be more to it than twenty minutes in the back of a Chevy, at least it provides a flash of naughty fun. And why not? Teenagers look to the generation over them as the ones who started the famous sexual revolution. Even between the years 1970 and 1980 the number of unmarried couples living together increased by 157.4 percent. In the thirty years between 1950 and 1980, the Kinsey Report shows that the number of kids who have had intercourse before their sixteenth birthdays has increased from 2 percent to 30 percent among the girls and from 10 percent to 50 percent among the boys. And we cannot boast about a record number of cases of venereal disease: 10 million, not to mention those who are suffering quietly, having yet to seek medical help.

Wayne Youngquist, sociologist at Marquette University, says "Most people today are in a state of 'betweenity.' They are caught between the new morality and the old...." And he warns, "A society that can't draw the line opens the way for normative collapse."

Suicide: The Final Painkiller

I still get surprised when teenagers get honest enough with me to tell me that they have thought seriously about suicide. In every youth group I have ever been associated with, I have always known of at least one who has thought about the benefits of being dead. If nothing else relieves pain, at least there is one final and sure way out.

A kid does not get there overnight. There is a long process that a person goes through to prefer death to life, but every suicide case has always had a common denominator: pain that person did not know how to respond to.

Even in a hospital, where bodies are failing, doctors and nurses know that there is still a chance as long as there is a will to live, but when the will to live is gone, the chances of survival are far less. What makes a faltering body give up? When the body is in such pain that the effort to function is considered worse than death, the will to live is gone. In the same way emotional, social, or mental pain can cause us to lose that same will to live. And from there it is not a big step to get a will to die.

You show me someone who has considered suicide, and I will show you someone who hurts. In fact frequently in counseling situations I will ask people who express deep bitterness and resentments in reaction to pain, "Have you ever thought of committing suicide?" They usually look back at me as if they were amazed that anyone besides themselves knew about it.

Is It All Relief?

We have seen how pain has driven many young lives to seek relief from these false painkillers, but can we say that all cocaine and teenage sex and alcoholism are the result of pain? Are all kids who smoke freebase or take Quaaludes or have one-night stands seeking relief from hard-core pain?

Well, there are 25 million teenagers in the United States, and they have indeed felt more pain than they have known how to handle. The pain has driven thousands, probably millions, into these fake painkillers. However we cannot say that 100 percent of the teenage marijuana smokers have faced some major crisis. Nor would we say that 100 percent of the sexually active teenagers have experienced a major family disaster. There are many who simply like the fellowship of beer or the fellowship of grass or the more intimate fellowship of sex. There are thousands of sincere young people who are convinced that virginity is a disease or, like an appendix, basically useless. They see everyone else turning on to the new drugs, and they follow unthinkingly. To be perfectly honest, they do experience certain pleasures. Getting drunk does loosen a person up and help him become less inhibited. However no one smokes grass week after week because life is high enough without it. And far fewer have premarital sex when they are receiving affection without it.

So even for the casually involved, these areas of activity do provide fun and thrills for an otherwise boring and often painful existence.

People Killers

The reason we have called these painkillers "fake" is because they eventually become people killers. Young people who have suffered under boredom or loneliness have been suckered into thinking that they are nearing the fountain of youth, when in fact they are in the gas chambers of Auschwitz. Rather than finding any lasting relief, they experience even deeper pain. For examples we can just flip through the prophets of our generation:

- Jimi Hendrix died at the age of twenty-seven of an overdose of sleeping pills. He took nine times the normal dosage.
- Keith Moon, funkie drummer of the Who, died in September 1978 of an overdose of sleeping pills.
- In 1969, Brian Jones, guitar player of the Rolling Stones, was found dead in his own swimming pool, under the influence of drugs.
- Jim Morrison, lead singer of the Doors, was buried in Paris, in July of 1971, before the cause of death was discovered.
- In 1979, Sid Vicious, of the Sex Pistols, died of a heroin overdose while on trial for the murder of his female friend.
- Duane Allman and Berry Oakley, both of the Allman Brothers Band, died from motorcycle crashes that took place within a mile of each other.

- Terry Kath, a member of the jazz-rock group Chicago, lifted a pistol to his head, in January 1978, killing himself instantly.
- Elvis Presley was found dead on his bathroom floor, in August 1977, with ten different drugs in his bloodstream.

Essentially a painkiller that causes more pain is a fake painkiller. A painkiller that numbs one area of my life while it eats away at another is a fake painkiller. Anything that offers only temporary relief while it causes lasting damage is a cheat, a fake.

"So What?"

"So what if I die young? I might be better off."

There are a lot of young people who are convinced that they are not worth saving. They look at the list of this generation's philosophers who have self-destructed, throw their moist Kleenexes in the air, and say, "See, life isn't worth nothin'!"

I had a friend in high school who would come to class on Monday mornings with elaborate stories of his weekend activities. His reckless escapades were hard for me to understand. He seemed heedless of dangers. He would think nothing of getting totally smashed and driving his car through the city streets, running red lights and paying no attention to speed limits. His other friends would have to remind him of the things he did, because he was too buzzed to remember. At the time his behavior confused me, but I shrugged my shoulders with a different-strokes-for-different-folks attitude. Now, looking back, I can see that the way he treated himself actually revealed the way he viewed life.

I once asked him, "What if there was a car in the intersection when you went through the red light?"

"Well," he smiled, "there wasn't."

His view of life reminded me of Joplin.

Janis Joplin, the queen of rock-and-roll in the late sixties, would chug a bottle of Southern Comfort on stage at concerts and was reported to be a heroin addict. When asked why she did not take better care of herself, she answered in typical fashion for people who have lost purpose in life: She admitted that taking care of her health might add a few years, but she didn't care. Those two or three years of life did not make much difference to Janis. What were they? twenty-four or thirty-six months of misery. Soon after she made that statement, she was found dead at twenty-seven. Near her was a red balloon filled with white powder—heroin. The coroner said she died of an overdose.

Here is the point: You do not gamble with life if it is of value to you. If you are treating your life carelessly, like an empty Budweiser can, you do not need a doctor to tell you the physical consequences of your life-style. You do not need a college professor explaining your psychological dilemma. You do not need any religious leader preaching morals. If you have ever been hurt so much that you would rather be numb and take the chance of dying than be alive and feel all that pain, then you do not need a sermon. You need someone to tell you that you are worth more than you think you are, because after you have been treated like a piece of junk for a while, you start seeing yourself as junk. A longer life is the last thing a hurting kid cares about.

I have talked with over 100 teenage alcoholics and drug addicts, but I have yet to find one who was glad at his condition. Many plead that they were innocent when they first got involved and were only looking for some peace of mind. Even though they knew that their habits might be self-destructive, at the time they really did not care.

There is actually some comfort gained from getting totally plastered. "Everybody else has kicked me and spit on me, so why can't I hurt myself?" And there is great satisfaction in the "fellowship of pain" when we get bombed with others who hurt. Parents scratch their heads in vain, wondering why we hang around with such "creeps." Sometimes they do not see what we have in common, because they do not see the pain. For many teens, the drugs and sex and booze are not as important as having someone with them who knows what it feels like.

"I Hate Myself!"

One of the most diabolical effects of these false painkillers is that they eventually cause us to hate ourselves.

Thomas "Hollywood" Henderson, former Dallas Cowboys linebacker, had a lot going for him as a football player. But after a dozen years of casual drug use, he started using a half ounce of cocaine a day and then graduated to freebasing cocaine (mixing cocaine and liquid ether, which gives a quicker high). He started to hate himself:

> Drugs just got me. When a person realizes that he has a problem, well, it's like if your arm stinks. You offend yourself first. I was doing it but I hated myself. I was beginning to be two people—the straight Thomas and the high "Hollywood." . . . The last five years it has been cocaine. I got up to doing a half ounce a day. That's terrible. I'm not proud of it . . . I'd like to ask people to pray for me. I need their prayers. I'm in a bad way, but I'm hanging in there.

Drugs can be killers, even when they only kill self-respect. As Henderson says, when there is something you hate about yourself, it is like dragging a rotten arm around with you all the time: It stinks!

Anybody Out There?

Pain paints a picture of God, and it is usually an ugly one. We might not consciously and immediately think about the Person who is supposedly in charge of our chaotic world, but eventually pain points its ugly finger upward and says, "It's His fault." Once we agree that it is indeed His fault, we have an ugly picture in our minds: Either He is like some fat-cat bureaucrat who egotistically bosses people around, or having let things get out of control, He, too, has run away and is probably sitting on some cloud, smoking a reefer. When our bodies and emotions hurt, our minds can draw incredible pictures of the thing we call God. Then after the picture is drawn, we usually crumple it up and throw it in the trash, leaving us in a closed universe without any God and without any purpose or meaning to life.

Pain looks for a way out. And since pain usually sees the doors of heaven slammed shut in its face, it does not look up for long and is therefore forced back to a temporary solution (a fake painkiller).

All of us, and millions of other teenagers just like us, have more than once lifted clenched fists toward heaven and cried, "Cram it!" For most of us, after the dust settles and our engines cool down, we sincerely wonder if there isn't more to life than what we see down here.

The Source of All Pain

All pain comes from one common source, and I hope you will hate that source with every cell in your body. Despite the fact that when we hurt, we often blame it on God, He is not the source of pain. As He originally created the world, there was no pain, no tears, and no disorder. Rather, the source of all pain is *sin*. That is right! The wages of sin is pain. Because we have turned the garden into a garbage heap, pain is a reality of life.

God promised Adam and Eve that if they ate of the tree of the forbidden fruit, they would surely die. They ate, and they started hurting. Eve hurt physically when childbirth pain was introduced. Sweat and blisters and backaches were experienced. They both hurt spiritually because they were no longer in fellowship with God. They hurt socially because they were cut off from each other and immediately blamed each other; later one of their sons killed the other. They hurt personally because they knew that they were guilty and tried to bear the burden by themselves.

Sin shows itself in many different ways, but it always hurts. If your heart has built up any resentment toward pain, I hope it will all be channeled into a pure hatred of sin.

We have already determined that Jesus is not a joy killer who runs around yelling, "Sinner," every time we start having fun. Rather He is a Painkiller who loves us too much to allow us to blindly lunge into the bear trap of temporal delights. Jesus loves you enough to hold you responsible for your own actions. If you have held fire to your breast, you have been burned (and you know what I am talking about).

Sin and pain are part of the diabolical plan of Satan. He was the intruder in God's creation, sowing seeds of sin that would produce crops of pain. Jesus called Satan a "murderer from the beginning" and the "father of lies" (John 8:44 RSV). The Bible says Satan relishes the slaughtering of his own children (Isaiah 14:20).

Satan has set a giant bear trap, baiting it with temporal delights and brilliantly disguising it. Even though we know the dangers, generation after generation falls victim and suffers the painful consequences. It is time that we recognize the source of all pain and find lasting relief.

Man of Sorrows

Even though you might hate the name *Jesus* as much as I hate lima beans, let me tell you something perhaps you never knew about Him.

Jesus knows what it is like to get hurt. In fact that may be the understatement of the century. Jesus is the most rejected, the most spit on, kicked around, and abused man who ever lived. He knows what it is like to have His close friends reject Him. Physically He was whipped, stabbed, tortured, and nailed. He has felt the sting of getting mocked in front of all His peers. He knows what it is like to leave home and to suffer the rejection of His Father.

The Picture Jesus Paints of God

Jesus has felt it all. There is hardly a pain that any of us will ever feel that Jesus has not already felt. But when Jesus suffered, He tried to tell us something. Primarily He wants us to know that He cares.

I have said that one of the ugliest things about growing up is feeling as if we have to do it all by ourselves. Pain makes things even worse, because when we hurt all alone, we are convinced that no one in the universe understands what we are going through and that no one cares.

There is only one problem: When Jesus hung on the cross, He smashed all that. He showed that *He* understands, and *He* cares.

Our suffering paints a picture of God, usually an ugly one. But when Jesus suffered, He painted a different picture of God, one that shows Him as being strangely compassionate and understanding. When we understand what happened when Jesus died, the face of God changes: His eyes change from cold steel to eyes of compassion mixed with tears; His mouth becomes friendly and understanding, rather than having a resentful frown or an apologetic smirk: His fists become open, nail-scarred hands inviting all who labor and are heavy laden to come to Him; and the fingers are taken from His ears, making Him a loving listener.

One evening my three-year-old son and I were washing our car. Since I only had a short hose, after I finished with one side, I had to turn the car around so that we could clean the other side. "You stay right here," I told my son, putting him safely out of the way. I turned the car around, and when I was backing up I heard a horrifying scream. I knew it was Fred. I threw the car into Park, flung the door open, and ran to locate the scream. At first I could not find him, I panicked. A few more throaty cries and I found him draped over and stuck to a prickly-pear cactus. (That was better than being under my tire.) It took me some time to get him loose. Finally with the majority of thorns picked from him, I held him close. That was all he wanted. He did not want any lectures about not doing what he was told. Those would come later. Words would have been terribly inappropriate. All he wanted was a strong but compassionate shoulder to cry on. Very quickly the tears stopped. He pushed himself far enough from my chest to look me in the eyes. A hint of a smile rose from his mouth as if to say, "Boy, am I glad you are my daddy!"

In much the same way, when we are overwhelmed with pain and suffering, as if stuck in some cactus, our Father comes to us and, if we will let Him, picks us up and offers us a tender, understanding shoulder on which to cry.

Will you repent? Will you turn from committing spiritual suicide to the One who is the Redeemer and the Life? Will you quit all pain-causing activities, which have only been destroying you, and let Jesus put your life back together again? Will you stop trying to get high synthetically and allow Jesus to teach you how to enjoy the natural highs of life?

Have you heard the message of the cross? Has it gotten under your skin to where it actually paints a more accurate picture of God?

Although you might have every good reason in the world for being involved in fake painkillers, Jesus loves you too much to let you continue. Let this be the day when the power of Christ's resurrection explodes in your life.

Have you heard the message of the cross? Has it gotten under your skin to where it actually paints a more accurate picture of God?

Although you might have every good reason in the world for being involved in fake painkillers, Jesus loves you too much to let you continue. Let this be the day when the power of Christ's resurrection explodes in your life.

14 Real Relief

I wish I could take an eraser and remove all your painful memories, but I can't. I wish I could give you an immediate solution to all your current problems, but I can't do that, either. However it is probably a good thing that I can't, because if I could, you would never grow up.

Hard Times
Jamie Owens
Is the rain fallin' from the sky
Keepin' you from singin'?
Is that tear fallin' from your eye
'Cause the wind is stingin'?

Chorus:
Well, don't you fret now, child,
Don't you worry;
The rain's to help you grow,
So don't try to hurry the storm along;
The hard times make you strong.

Don't you know a seed could never grow
If there were never showers?
And though the rain might bring a little pain,
Just look at all the flowers!

Chorus
I know how long a day can seem
When storm clouds hide His face;
And if the rain dissolves your dream,
Just remember His amazin' grace.

Don't you know the sun is always there
Even when the rains fall?

And don't you know the Son will always care
When He hears your voice call?

Growth or Death

No one was ever born with calluses. The bottoms of babies' feet
are as soft as Jell-O and the palms of their hands are like marsh-
mallows. As a child develops, the knees are usually the first place to
show signs of wear. In junior high, those baby feet often bleed with
blisters after basketball practice. In high school and college they
build up thick protective skin so they can withstand physical punishment. Calluses on our bodies are okay.

Unfortunately, as we grow up and suffer emotional punishment,
we often build up internal calluses. There is one big problem: Thick
skin is dead skin. It is one thing for the outer layer of our bodies to
die; but when our inner selves die, then we are in trouble.

Without question the most helpful and maturing process I had
while in high school was when I almost died from the concussion I
described earlier. Oh, I had fun playing on the all-county baseball
team, winning medals running track, being involved in student government and attending the senior prom. But these fun, exciting
things did not cause me to develop and mature the way my near-
fatal concussion did.

As I lay in the hospital room, I questioned, panicked, screamed,
cried, argued, and almost gave up. Later, when I was told that I
would never play football again, I felt as if something had died. For
me the commonplace occurrence—a football injury—produced
hard-core pain. I built up a thick callus on my heart, which would
protect me from ever again being hurt with such disappointment.
But then my perspective changed, and that single most painful experience eventually led me to learn, grow, mature, and to find God.

Rather than leading to death, it actually brought vitality and growth.

Napoleon Bonaparte, France's macho military leader, perceptively stated, "It required more courage to suffer than to die."

Yes, when we get hurt, it is easier to die internally than to suffer and grow. Both *common pain* and *hard-core pain* can become *growing pains.*

Respect Myself

When we do not respond properly, pain can cause us to hate ourselves, but when we do respond properly, it will cause us to grow in self-respect.

Glenn was only eight years old when he was severely burned in a household fire. This horrifying experience left him without any toes on his left foot and with very little muscle tissue on either leg. The doctors told Glenn that he would probably never walk again.

This crisis could have dealt a death blow to this young boy, but Glenn said he was too young to die. Through dedication and hard work he began to walk. He was not satisfied by developing his leg muscles through exercise, so he determined that he would run.

In high school he went out for the track team and excelled with such resolve that Glenn Cunningham was the fastest school-age miler in the United States. While attending the University of Kansas, in 1934 he set the world record of 4:06.8 in the mile run.

Glenn Cunningham did not let childhood pain hinder his personal development. His very serious hard-core pain became a *growing pain,* and from it he gained tremendous self-respect.

Youth can be a time when we get hurt and then wander off into some corner and lick our wounds. Some teenagers are experts at self-pity. But it does not have to be that way. The same pain that could potentially drive us deep within ourselves can also teach us that we are still worthwhile. We need to realize that we are bigger than whatever hurts us. While self-pity drives us into a corner where we feel very small, self-respect calls us out and makes us feel important and worthwhile.

Respect Others

A negative response to pain will leave us with a low view of human life, but a proper response to pain will teach us to have a very high regard for life.

None of our contemporaries stands out as a better example of a positive response to teenage pain than Joni Eareckson. It all happened this way:

The hot July sun was setting low in the west and gave the waters of Chesapeake Bay a warm red glow. The water was murky, and as my body broke the surface in a dive, its cold cleanness doused my skin.

In a jumble of action and feelings, many things happened simultaneously. I felt my head strike something hard and unyielding. At the same time, clumsily and crazily, my body sprawled out of control. I heard or felt a loud electric buzzing, an unexplainable inner sensation. It was something like an electrical shock, combined with a vibration—like a heavy metal spring being suddenly and sharply uncoiled, its "sprong" perhaps muffled by the water. Yet it wasn't really a sound or even a feeling—just a sensation. I felt no pain.

I heard the underwater sound of crunching, grinding sand. I was lying face down on the bottom. *Where? How did I get here? Why are my arms tied to my chest?* My thoughts screamed. *Hey! I'm caught! . . .*

Panic seized me. With all my will power and strength, I tried to break free. Nothing happened. Another tidal swell lifted and rolled.

What's wrong? I hit my head. Am I unconscious? . . . But I'll drown! . . .

I felt the pressure of holding my breath begin to build. I'd have to breath soon. . . .

I'm going to die! I don't want to die! Help me, please. . . .

"Joni!" That voice! Muffled through the waters, it sounded far off. Now it was closer. "Joni, are you all right?"

Kathy! My sister sees me. Help me, Kathy! I'm stuck! . . .

Her shadow indicated she was now above me. I struggled inwardly against panic, but I knew I had no more air. Everything was going dark.

I felt Kathy's arms around my shoulders, lifting.

Oh, please, dear God. Don't let me die!

Kathy struggled, stumbled, then lifted again. *Oh, God, how much longer?* Everything was black, and I felt I was falling while being lifted. Just before fainting, my head broke the water's surface. *Air!* Beautiful, life-giving, salt-tinged air. I choked in oxygen so quickly, I almost gagged. Gasping, I gulped in mouthfuls. . . .

I looked down at my chest. My arms were not tied. I realized with a growing terror that my limbs were dangling motionlessly. I couldn't move them!

This was only the beginning of a very painful process for Joni Eareckson, a process she is still living with. She has never regained the mobility she lost that afternoon. She will never ride a horse or go swimming on her own again. She went from being a very normal teenager to having some of the most severe limitations possible. She went through the phases of hard-core pain in which she cursed life and wished she were dead.

Today, although the severity of her situation has not changed, her attitudes have changed, and her pains have helped her grow. From her wheelchair she has spoken to millions about the maturing process of misery. Today she heads a group called Joni and Friends, which seeks to reach out and help other disabled people through their difficulties. Her own sorrow has made her sensitive to those around her, and she has blossomed because of her growing pains.

Respect For God

Hard-core pain raises its angry fist toward heaven, but growing pain realizes that He's not the One to blame.

Joni Eareckson went through a period of resenting God, but when she recognized that He was a Man of Sorrows and knew what it was like to be paralyzed, she was able to respond to Jesus as a personal Friend. Her friendship with Jesus grew so personal that she writes, "I had no other identity but God, and gradually He became enough." God spoke to Joni out of the midst of tragedy and got her undivided attention. He spoke to her about the ultimate concerns of life: "The peace that counts is an inner peace, and God has lavished me with peace." As a paraplegic, she longs for heaven; "Being glorified—I know the meaning of that now. It's the time after my death here, when I'll be on my feet dancing."

My grandmother is an example of growing pain. Everyone who knows her says there is no one as loving and self-sacrificing as she. She is constantly giving of herself to others, but for those who know her best she stands out for her sincere love for God. She has a genuine humility and gratitude to God for His goodness to her. She prays in very simple, childlike faith to her Father who has done so much more for her than she ever deserved. What only those in her immediate family know is that her mother died when she was born.

When she was old enough to realize that her mother had given her life for her, it hurt. Although her father showed her tremendous love, as others did, she never forgot the fact that someone gave her life for her, right from the start. That childhood pain, which could have sent many into bitterness and resentment, placed a wound in my grandmother's heart that has poured forth extraordinary love to God and others around her.

Hatred of Sin

We have seen how sin is the source of all pain. It has been part of God's perfect plan for us to feel the sting of sin until we hate it with intense passion. We have all felt the sting of sin, and we all need to recognize it as the diabolical enemy of mankind.

Can you remember the last time you vomited? If you remember what you ate right before regurgitating, chances are you hate that particular food. I have a friend who ate Chinese food the night be-

fore he got the flu. Although there was probably no relationship between the food and the flu, since that is what he saw land between
his legs when he heaved, he still cannot eat Chinese food.

The first time I can remember getting sick to my stomach, I had
just finished eating meat loaf. I dismissed myself from the table,
walked outside and lost it. . . . I went inside to bed, woke up the next
morning feeling 100 percent better, but for years after that even the
smell of meat loaf cooking was enough to make me sick. It made
every muscle in my body go into spasms just to hear the words *meat
loaf.*

In the same way we need to loathe sin. Sin is more than sicken-
ing; it is a killer, and the thought of it should make us recoil in hor-
ror. It is an enemy of life and the sole source of every trace of pain
we have ever felt. May Proverbs 26:11 (RSV) be true for none of us,
"Like a dog that returns to his vomit is a fool that repeats his folly."
As we grow through pain, we will grow to hate sin.

No More Self-pity

Rather than sitting in the corner, licking our wounds, or walking
around with armored plates strapped to us, which say, "Stay away,
I'm cold and hardened," we have another option. We can allow
those sore spots of life to teach us. It does not matter where the pain
comes from—inferiority, parents, dating, conscience, boredom, or
whatever—it always gives us an opportunity to grow.

One of the most outstanding athletes of all times was Emil Zato-
pek, a Czechoslovakian who stood out in the 1952 Olympic Games,
in which he won three gold medals and held several world records.
He trained by running more than six hours every day. He said of his
training, "I run until I hurt; that's when I begin my training program . . . I've learned that if I can just get beyond fatigue, there is a
reserve of power that I never dreamed I had, and then I go on and
run my best races."

In a sense the training program of life begins when things start to
hurt. That is where we start to learn and grow and mature. Obviously only masochists enjoy pain, but Christians can see the po-

tential in pain. It can push us within ourselves to where we want to quit, or it can push us beyond ourselves to where we want to win.

When you hurt, you never need to be alone. Jesus invites you to Himself:

> Come unto me, all ye that labour and are heavy laden, and I will give you rest. Take my yoke upon you, and learn of me; for I am meek and lowly in heart: and ye shall find rest unto your souls. For my yoke is easy, and my burden is light.

Matthew 11:28-30 KJV

1. Why is it easy to blame God when we hurt?
2. Why is it wrong to blame God when we hurt? What should we blame?
3. Why can Jesus help us when we hurt?
4. What is repentance?
5. Think about a painful experience you have had. What effect has it had on your life? How can that help you to mature?
6. Through the book we have seen how Jesus can help us deal with pain. If you let Him, how can He make a difference for you?

1. According to the author, what causes kids to get heavily into alcohol, drugs, sex, and even to consider suicide? Do you agree
   with him?
2. Why are "fake painkillers" fake?
3. Discuss the statement "life is cheap."
4. What are the two basic ways people respond to pain?
5. What are some things Joni Eareckson has learned that we all
   need to learn?
6. List five specific qualities included in the word *maturity*.